The Keys to Success
on the Road Less Traveled

Terry Sprouse, editor

Planeta Books, LLC
Tucson, Arizona

Copyright ©2017 by Terry Sprouse.

All rights reserved. Printed in the United States of America. Except as permitted under the United States Copyright act of 1976, no part of this book may be reproduced or transmitted in any form or by any means, electronic or mechanical, including photocopying, recording, or by any information storage or retrieval system, without written permission from the copyright holder, except for the inclusion of quotations in a review.

ISBN 978-0-9798566-8-6

This publication is designed to provide accurate and authoritative information in regard to the subject matter covered. It is provided with the understanding that neither the author nor the publisher is engaged in rendering legal, accounting or other professional services. If legal or other expert assistance is required, the services of a competent professional person should be sought.

Published by:
Planeta Books, LLC
Tucson, Arizona

For updates and more resources visit:

www.TerrySprouse.com

Contents

Acknowledgements 5
Introduction 7

1. Attitude and Self-esteem

Always Choose Love and Happiness 10
    Andres Ruiz
Love You 16
    Barb Hildenbrand
Dead Man's Cliff, No More 21
    Thomas Kanspedos

2. Overcoming Obstacles

Love Your Life 26
    Michael Sorantino
Finding Stories on Your Hero's Journey 32
    Terry Sprouse
Henry Ford - Keys to Success 37
    David Smith
Success While Waiting 44
    Darrell Parrish Bakeman

3. Special Moments

Man's Best Friend 52
    John Grand

Marching Band on the Street 57
    Yontaek Choi
Viewing Life Through Poetry 61
    Arthur G. Lohman
Disobedience Pays Off 75
    Philip Schultz

4. Live Your Dream

Why Do I Still Teach? 80
    Myrna P. Fileccia
My Toastmasters Journey.. 85
    Randy Casarez
From Woes to Wins with Three Action Types 89
    Raleigh Ormerod
License to Thrill 98
    James Babcock

Author Biographies 105

Acknowledgements

Thank you to James Babcock and Rich Konkle for their superlative cover design. Also, thank you to Randy Casarez for his insightful input on the book title.

Introduction

What is success?

Our society usually associates the accumulation of financial wealth with being successful. Our culture is replete with biased expressions glorifying wealth.

"She really made something of herself?"

"He has the Midas touch."

"I feel like a million bucks!"

Yet, being successful in life is more than money. One definition of the word 'successful' is 'fruitful.' To me, that broadens the meaning to give us a fuller perspective. It changes the color of the word from black and white to technicolor.

In the following chapters, the authors illustrate the different shades and colors of the word 'success.' We view success as: realigning one's life following the death of a loved one; channeling the energy of rejection into writing comic books; recognizing the daunting sacrifices of one's mother; finding inspiration in working with disadvantaged youth; recognizing the trials of being a teacher; celebrating the nobility of 'man's best friend;' capturing the essence of life through the lens of poetry; overcoming the past and finding ways to love yourself; among many other intriguing ways.

The title of this book, *The Keys to Success on the Road Less Traveled*, refers to the subtle insight that we glean from reflecting on the experiences of life, and embracing the nuances of meaning that life presents to us.

The authors of this book are all members of *Toastmasters* Clubs, and all are skilled public speakers. If you would like to know more about their topic, or to schedule them to speak, feel free to contact them. Their contact information is found in their biography.

You are in for a rare treat. The following chapters will inspire, teach and motivate you to hopefully find your own definition of success. If you don't find one inside yourself, just borrow one of ours!

As Albert Schweitzer said, "Success is not the key to happiness. Happiness is the key to success. If you love what you are doing, you will be successful."

Terry Sprouse

1
Attitude and Self-esteem

When we are no longer able to change a situation, we are challenged to change ourselves.

Viktor Frankl

Always Choose Love and Happiness
Andres Ruiz

"You must be willing to sacrifice who you are for what you will become."

These are the words I heard from the great motivational speaker, Eric Thomas, as I was sitting at my desk at a job that I hated. I stood up and walked directly to my supervisor and asked if I could speak with her in private. She had a look of concern when she saw my serious face.

When we sat down in the private room, we had the following conversation:

"Mary, I am putting in my two-week notice," I told her. She gave me a look of shock.

"Are you sure you want to put in your two-week notice? You've been here for four years and the pay is good," she said, with a look as if I was crazy.

"Yes, I am sure," I said.

I honestly was not sure of what I was doing. Although I was uncertain of what the future held for me, I was happy that I finally left a job that was making me miserable.

Did you know that over 70 percent of people in the United States hate their job? After I quit my job I began researching motivational speaking. I was determined to be a public speaker. I'd heard about a club called *Toastmasters*. I went on the internet to look at the *Toastmasters* website. I found a phone number for a club called *Southwest Toastmasters* and spoke to a very nice woman by the name of Karen Hebda. She was very sweet and welcoming and so were the club members. I immediately decided to join the club, and I gave my first speech within a couple of weeks.

I also remember going to an auditorium to watch a speech contest. It was amazing to see motivational speakers on stage inspiring the audience. I looked at the stage and told myself, "I will be on that stage very soon." Four months later, I was on that same stage competing in a speech contest.

"We become what we think about," said Earl Nightingale.

The man was absolutely right. The mind will believe anything you say to it. The mind is like a farmer's land. If the farmer plants a seed of corn, it will give corn and if he plants a seed of nightshade, which is venom, the land will give venom. You see, the land does not care what you plant. It will return venom in just as wonderful abundance as it will corn. That's how the human brain works. It does not care if you plant a seed of positivity, like the corn, or a seed of negativity, like venom. It will give you whichever you plant. If you plant your dream, that seed will also become a reality, if you picture it every day.

I remember years ago, when I was very negative and depressed. I weighed 265 pounds, drank alcohol, and ate unhealthy foods like there was no tomorrow. I knew that what I was doing was bad for my health, but I did not care because I did not love myself. When you don't love yourself, you don't care what you put into your body. I would feel sad and I would look to alcohol or food to make me happy. I would drink all night to numb my pain until I passed out and woke up feeling worse. I would eat fast foods to help me get over my hangover. The alcohol and unhealthy food would take away the pain temporarily, but then the depression would always come back. I kept this pattern going for many years.

I was then blessed to find out I was going to be a father. I told myself I must change my lifestyle because if I don't take care of myself, who is going to take care of my son? I joined some weight loss competitions, started exercising and eating healthy foods. The transformation I saw my body go through was incredible. I went from weighing 265 pounds to 185 pounds. I felt in the best shape of my life and I still do at age 33. I feel healthier than when I was in my early 20's. Losing 80 pounds was the second best thing to happen to me, right behind the birth of my son.

I felt like a new person with more confidence. I noticed how much happier I was and how I could run around with my son without feeling out of breath. If I had not lost the weight, I would never have considered being a motivational speaker. Being overweight made me self-conscious about myself. I worried that people would judge me because of my physique. After leaving my job, I began exploring other jobs that piqued my interest. Let's just say I found a few more jobs that I hated as much as the prior one I had.

I then found a job at a shelter that I loved. Working at a shelter humbles you like you could never imagine. This job really opened my eyes on how fortunate I was. These kids were 13-17 years old with challenging experiences in their lives. We sometimes complain about petty things like not having a nice car, when there are people out there walking miles back and forth to work, just to be able to get a meal for the day. We complain about our looks when we should feel blessed to have our health. There are many people in this world who do not have their health, yet they are still more positive than people who have their health.

The kids at the shelter had to grow up fast at an early age because of their circumstances. They had experiences that no young child should go through. I taught the kids about affirmations and self-motivation so that they could believe in themselves.

"Tell yourself, *I believe in myself*," I would say to them every day. I told them that if they don't believe in themselves, nobody else will.

After just a few weeks, I loved these kids like little brothers and sisters. I also felt that they loved me just by the way they treated me and the experiences they shared with me. They would make bracelets out of yarn by hand. I got a lot of bracelets from the boys and girls. That was their way of showing their appreciation for what I did for them. Every day I would get compliments from the boys and girls that they really appreciated me motivating them and inspiring them. That was worth more than the money I was being paid. When you are doing something that you love, the money does not matter. What matters most is the feeling you get in your heart just by serving others.

By service I mean that smile you leave on people's faces, that memory that will stay with them forever. When one of the kids would leave the shelter it was as if a family member left. It's amazing how in just a few months you can create a strong bond with someone. That just shows us how grateful we should feel for having our family. Just like that young child who left the shelter, one day it will be our own child leaving our house and going out to venture into the world.

Can you imagine being with your family one day, and the next not being able to see them? Even worse, imagine not seeing them for years. I was speaking to one of the kids who had not seen his family in almost a year. He talked to me about how his family relied on him to work and provide food for his two little brothers and his mother. He told me one night that he spoke to his mother on the phone and she was very upset. She blamed him for his family starving because he was not working to provide for them. He also told me that his two little brothers, who were nine and ten years old, were working to provide for the family and that he felt guilty because he was not there to help them out.

He would throw away his food, because he felt guilty that his family could not eat, and he could. I told him that he had to eat and take care of himself, so that when he left the shelter he could start working again to help out his family. He told me he was very thankful to have me in his life and he began crying. I was trying to stay strong and not cry but I couldn't help it. It was as if one of my own kids was crying. I couldn't hold back the tears anymore, and they just flowed down my cheek.

There were two guys who worked at the shelter that were looking at me. I said, "DAMN!!" I laughed, thinking these dudes just saw me crying. As men, we are not allowed to cry, because we are expected to be tough. We hold it in until we feel like somebody has been choking us for a couple of minutes. You know that feeling when you try really hard to hold in the tears but you just can't help but cry? Then you try to wipe the tears before anybody sees you, but you know everyone saw you. They just turn away.

We must be thankful for what we have instead of complaining about what we don't have. Many of us here in the United States have a lot to be thankful for, but we just take it for granted. Take a moment to close your eyes for a few minutes and think of a person that is in your life at this moment that you are grateful for because they make you happy. Think about a happy moment that you and that person shared and the great feeling you got in your heart just by having that experience. After doing this, contact that person, and talk to them about that experience you had with them. This whole process will just take a few minutes, or more depending on how long you talk to that person.

I guarantee you will be happy that whole time. You will be expressing gratitude for that person, which will make them express gratitude towards you because you made their day at that moment. Always remember to live in the moment, not in the past or the future.

We must be happy and full of energy, so we can make others happy. This is what life is all about. Life is about making others happy, giving to others the reaction of happiness and putting a big smile on their face. That is worth more than gold, or any material things that we sometimes appreciate more than our loved ones and our health. When we follow our dreams, it often opens doors to other dreams and aspirations we never allowed ourselves to even think of before. Once I started giving motivational speeches, I then decided that I would like to explore becoming a life coach. Because of the success I had in the speaking realm, it suddenly seemed possible. I have since developed a web site and blog, and I have several clients with whom I work, serving as their life coach. The possibilities are endless!

Singer Al Green said it best, "It is all about love and happiness." Think about something you've always wanted to do and sacrifice who you are at this very moment, so you can pursue what you will be in the future. Always choose love and never let fear stop you from being the person you must become. You have unlimited potential. Give your love away and make the world a better place!

Love You

Barb Hildenbrand

How do I love me, let me count the ways ... Oh, isn't that how it goes?

I have been thinking a lot recently about how we treat those we love. Usually, the ones we love most, we treat the worst. In contemplating this, I was reminded of a statement I have heard John Maxwell make numerous times, "You can't give what you don't have". Therefore, if you do not love *yourself*, and treat *yourself* well, you will be hard pressed to truly love others and treat them well.

I have three tips to help you love yourself more, which I hope you will consider, take to heart and take action upon:

#1-Don't let what **you have done** in the past define who you are today.

We all have done things that we are not proud of. Some of us have done things we consider unforgivable. We have said things that can't be taken back, as much as we wish we could.

Each day is a new day; we get to make choices each day, choices anew! We are able to change the direction we are headed by making a choice to change.

I have a soon-to-be nephew-in-law, who recently said,

Four years ago today I entered the treatment center a broken man and not knowing what to do with his life, or how much of a life he had left.

Today God has freed me from all drugs, he has given me the best fiancé a man could ask for, and a wonderful step son. I now have a purpose. Thank God I am not the man I used to be.

This young man was able to get over his past. He was only 24 years old when he made this statement. He felt broken... at 24 years of age! Of course he got help- sometimes ... many times, that is the best thing you can do for yourself. There is help available, so go get it if needed! If you don't know where to go, start asking.

This young man loves himself now! He is now able to love others and has found a fabulous family who loves him dearly!

#2-Don't let what **someone else said or did** in the past, hold you captive.

Can we all agree, life isn't perfect? For some, life was, or is pure hell. Most of us, maybe during our childhood, or as an adult, have experienced some sort of abuse. Have you suffered at the hand of someone else? Maybe verbal abuse? Physical abuse? Sexual abuse? More people than would like to admit, have been the victim of abuse.

Again, each day is a new day. *Choose* to take your life back. Do not let that person, those people or that past keep you imprisoned! Break free of their hold on you!

A friend has been taking a money course. Here is what she said, somewhat paraphrased:

For the last month or so I have been taking this money course. It was so eye opening. I had to deal with a lot of emotions that I had hidden as a child, but it was wrapped into my manifesting in money. We were given an affirmation to say daily and this morning it hit so hard, after 30 days of saying it, I got an anxiety attack. I stopped and breathed into it, and held my forehead and said I am safe.

Then I remembered the comments that were said to me when I was around 5 or 6, and then it hit me. That at 28 years old I was told by my boss if I wanted people to take me seriously and stop being so immature and irresponsible, I needed to drop the name of Roxie as it was a childish name, a theater and a hooker's name. I, at that point, took on my legal name of Roxanne. I now realize I saw myself as an awful person with that name; especially when he said a hooker, because of my sexual abuse as a child.

*So, today I went to the mirror and said I love you Roxie, I really, really love you Roxie! And I started smiling and laughing. It was like a heavy cloud was lifted. I can be me. I am so thankful I took this course. It has opened me up to accepting **myself** so much*

I love Roxie's Story! You never know who or what will speak to you. She was taking a money course! Be open to help you find your true self and free you from your past.

Choose to change. Allow yourself to let go of whatever happened in the past. If you need help - get it! But let it go and don't let it hold you captive any longer! That is a prison in which you do not belong.

#3- Don't let **current circumstances** keep you from moving forward.

What is holding you back? How is your self-talk? Is your home your sanctuary? Are *you* your biggest obstacle?

I have found recently that having areas in my house that are a mess, with piles (My name is Barb, and I am a stacker) and disorganization, were stealing energy from me. Not only that, but when I entered these areas, my self-talk would immediately turn to negative and deprecating language. Have you heard this type of talk from yourself?

"You are such a loser. You can't get your act together. Look, you can't even find what you need because of this mess ... **you** are a mess! Who do you think you are?"

Please listen carefully to what you say to yourself. When you hear this type of language... change it immediately! What is your first thought when I ask you, "Who do you think you are? (Pause here. Stop reading and think about it). What was your first thought? Did you have a positive thought? My thoughts were always negative. One of my business coaches, because he knows my faith, told me, every time I answer this question- answer it with, "I am a child of God!"

How will you answer this question? If you are a person of faith, you should answer the question with, "I am a child of God!" If you are not, feel free to use another answer, just make sure it is positive.

Don't allow any negative in your answer. You are awesome! You are an amazing human being with a lot to offer this world, and your fellow human beings.

What you say to yourself is so powerful! Your brain is designed to believe what it hears. I am sure you have heard the acronym GIGO - garbage in garbage out. I encourage you to change that to GOOD in good out. Remember, you can't give what you don't have. You must put good in, to get good out.

I also want to address the stackers out there. Many of us are so busy that we don't take time to keep ourselves organized; then we end up with the catch-all places in our homes and offices which create angst and steal our energy.

Take those places back as well. Take just 15 minutes at a time and decide that you will tackle just one area. Take, say, just the left side of the desk/table which is full of piles and stuff.

After the 15 minutes have passed, stop and give yourself a pat on the back for the great job you've just accomplished!

I encourage you today to begin taking your life back from the past, or the present, and correct that self-talk.

You are *no longer* that person who did or said what you did in the past.

You are *no longer* that person who was victimized by another.

You are *no longer* that person you have been telling yourself you are.

Feel free to create and say aloud a daily affirmation. You are amazing! You are not a mistake or an accident! You are loveable! You are a wonderfully made person who was put on this earth to love and be loved!

I love you and, I hope, you LOVE YOU!

Dead Man's Cliff, No More

Thomas Kanspedos

It was dark and the path leading up the wooded hillside was steep.

The going was tough and the precious cargo of two cases of Iron City beer was getting heavy. But we were young men in our teens and were up to the challenge. Soon we would be at our destination on a high ridge overlooking the Ohio River, perched on a huge rock that jutted out from the side of the cliff. Oh yes we were there, *Dead Man's Cliff*. The lights of the city of Pittsburgh and the river below, as far as the eye could see, provided a spectacular view.

We were in our little sanctuary, away from the world, away from parents, police and all figures of authority who could rain on our parade. A place where we could be as bad and wild as we wanted. We could smash our beer bottles on the rocks or stand on the edge of the cliff and throw our empties as far as we could into the darkness and beat our chest with a Tarzan yell.

Dead Man's Cliff was a place of intrigue. I remember the many times sitting on this very cliff when I was younger and listening to the older boys tell stories of the many grown-ups who lost all hope and took the fatal plunge to the rocks far below. It all made perfect sense. This was the perfect place for suicide, if there ever was one.

The party was in full gear, the beer was going down and the spirits were being lifted when Bones stood up (and yes, Bones got his name by his small and slim frame - he was usually the first one drunk), threw his head back, put the bottle to his mouth and guzzled the contents. With a Tarzan yell, he reared back and pitched the bottle as far as he could. But when he did he lost his footing and began to fall forward off the cliff, Mac quickly jumped up in a valiant attempt to save his friend. Mac grabbed Bones' arm but it was too late, in an instant they both vanished from the rock.

Was this real? Two friends gone in an instant?

Those of us who remained had no plan but to drink more beer. Then, a very strange thing happened. I heard voices behind me laughing. It sounded like Mack and Bones. I looked back and there they were, cracking open a cold one.

How did they cheat death?

It turns out that they fell into the thick vines and landed on a small ledge and followed it until they were able climb out. At first, a sense of relief filled me. Then, a second emotion began to take hold of me, a light went on in my head.

"Dead Man's Cliff, my eye," I thought.

I was duped.

It was all a fabricated story fed to me ever since I was a little kid. It was a bunch of crap and I had believed it, all of it. Yet, all the evidence was there. The high drop, the rocks down below, and the launching point from the rock that jutted out.

The problem was that I believed false information and never questioned it because I was so young.

"What other crap has been feed me when I was young that is not true?" I asked myself.

A few days later, when I returned to the cliff and looked down, I saw a view that I never saw before. Oh sure, there were still the rocks and I suppose that if a person jumped out head first and hit the rocks, death was a sure possibility.

But now I saw the view from a new perspective. I saw the thick vines and the lush foliage and it dawned on me that a person could go over the cliff and cheat death if they fell in the right place.

So what changed?

The cliff hadn't changed, but I had changed my belief in what I saw from the perspective of the rock which I was standing on.

I realized that we don't always see things as they are. Instead, we see things as we are.

What about going to a dysfunctional elementary school, where I was told that I was lazy and unmotivated and the school staff chose intimidation and humiliation to "help me" overcome my learning disability?

One interpretation might be, that instead of helping me, the school was only grooming me for a prison cell. Little boys, like me, who have been mistreated respond with anger, and lash out against the system.

Or I could, and did, choose to believe that being pushed off that cliff in elementary school did not kill my spirit. Instead, it instilled in me the will, and gave me a reason and the personal testimony, to reach down and give a hand; to look another struggling individual in the eye and say with confidence,

"I made it and so will you."

The question is, "What is your Dead Man's Cliff? What do you believe about yourself that is not true, even though you have eaten it up for years?"

Examine every negative and harmful thought that is in your head. Carefully contemplate who put it there, and why.

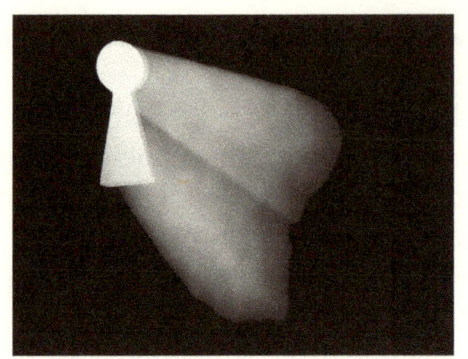

2
Overcoming Obstacles

Put your heart, mind, and soul into even your smallest acts. This is the secret of success.

Swami Sivananda

Love Your Life
Michael Sorantino

When I was about seven years old, my father died from a heart attack. He was a man in his mid-30s with a wife and 4 children. He had, what we now recognize as, an unhealthy lifestyle. But at the time, he was living a very normal life. He was a meat and potatoes kinda guy. He was the primary operator of a family business started by his father. And like most family businesses, the dysfunction of the family created lots of challenges in the business. The stress of this wore on him every day of his short life. He was a popular and well-liked guy, an active member of the *Rotary Club*, and I understand that his funeral was quite an event in our little town in southern New Jersey.

But frankly I don't really know much about him from my own experience or memory. Most of us are familiar with stories of those who have passed and how the accounts often take on a quality more like folklore than truth. I have one of those stories about him that happened for me shortly before he died. There was this father-son camping and canoeing trip in Canada. He was taking my two bothers and wanted to take me too, but both the trip organizers and my mother dug in saying that I was too young. But somehow he worked it out and I got to go. One of the nights we were camping on a small remote island and a bear must have smelled the food and swam across from another island. There was a big ruckus in our camp as the bear was rummaging through our stuff. In my mind, my father jumped up and fought the bear... and won. All I have is a picture in my mind the shadowy figure of my dad waving a stick and screaming and the seeing this huge bear running away. I'm sure there's more to it than that, but you get the idea and this is the image of my father that was frozen in my mind forever.

But this story isn't really about him. This story is more about what he left behind. He left a family. And each of us have lived a life that's been profoundly influenced by his absence. For each of us kids, there's a unique yet familiar story of loss – a loss of security, of guidance, of acknowledgement. These are things that, for better or for worse, come with the territory of having lost our father at a young age. But for me at least, there is also a story of growth and discovery, of self-reliance and success. These are all things that have a huge impact on who I am today as I'm sure all of my siblings would admit if they were able to be clear and honest about the situation.

But this story isn't about me or my siblings either. The person at the center of this story is my mother. This was a woman raised in a strict and traditional patriarchal Italian-American family in the 50s. She had to rebel against her father just to pursue a post high school education. And for a woman raised in the Wally Cleaver generation, this took serious resolve. She was the Homecoming Queen, May Queen, Miss Noel, captain of the cheerleading squad, and a Delaware Junior Golf Championship medalist. She seemed to get lots of attention for her physical prowess. I've seen pictures and she possessed the ideal look for a woman of her time and got a lot of attention for it. There was a picture taken of her and me that made the front page of the local newspaper. It was a silhouette of us walking down the aisle on my first day of kindergarten. I think the photographer was interested.

As typical for the times, she moved from her father's house to my father's house. She was never allowed to spend even one night outside her home growing up because, in my grandfather's words "you have a perfectly good bed here." She and my father built a $17,000 home with a 17% mortgage interest rate. She and my father got married and had 4 children, all spaced more or less 3 years apart. They had 3 boys and a baby girl... life was on track. I could go on, but I think you get the picture.

And then, one night they were out dancing and my father dropped out of my mother's arms and died right there on the dance floor.

With no time to consider what had just happened, she had to go home and face her four children of 3, 7, 10, and 13 years old. She had to somehow explain to us that Dad wasn't coming home ever again. I don't remember how she did that or my reaction to it, but I'm sure it must have been a surreal moment. I know that from that point on, every time she left the house I would cry out of fear that she wouldn't come home. I had this deep feeling in my gut that if she died too, I'd have no one left.

This woman somehow pulled herself together and carried on. She's told me the story of her going to her father and crying to him saying, "I don't know if I can do this." To this he simply responded, "You don't have a choice." and he dismissed her. This wasn't exactly the compassionate and sympathetic response she was looking for, but with the clarity that comes with many subsequent years of life, she came to realize the extraordinary wisdom in his approach; that this was exactly what she needed to hear and feels great admiration and gratitude toward her father.

Now this is a woman who came from a blue collar immigrant family. Her father was a golf course superintendent and both her brothers earned their living as construction laborers. All good, honest, hard-working people, but she was the only one who was determined to break out and reach toward her potential. There was something in her that drove her.

But when she married my father, she settled into the life that her father told her was her purpose – be a mother and a home-maker. I have a feeling that life presents all people with exactly what they need to become who they are destined to become. My father's death, while apparently tragic, pushed her back into the world and presented her with the opportunity to achieve more.

This woman began a career in selling real estate. It was the only path she could see that gave her an income and the flexibility to care for four children as a single parent. She was faced with incredible adversity in these initial years after my father's death. So much so that it reached into absurdity. My father's family, instead of being supportive of her through this process, took the family business from her and ran it into the ground. They even asked her for her wedding ring back to which she responded, "You will only take this ring off my dead hand."

My mother survived two bouts with cancer, two knee replacements, and survived an exploratory laparoscopy and oophorectomy. Through all this, my mother loved me and gave me everything she had to give. She gave of herself so profoundly, that there is no question of the unity of a mother and child. I'm sure she can't tell you where she ends and her children begin. We are all part of her energy field. And when any human can experience love like this, it demonstrates the potential for the unity of all humans.

Through all this, my mother was a prolific and successful real estate agent. She put her four children through college and gave us all the opportunity and skills we needed to succeed as well as a solid example of how to approach the inevitable adversity of life. "There are no excuses and you don't really have a choice." Through hard work, attention to detail, and undying integrity she was eventually recognized as a leader and moved into the management team of real estate offices.

At the age of 65, she took a risk and joined a couple young entrepreneurs to establish three new offices of an up and coming real estate firm. They built them from the ground up. They became the fastest growing offices in the franchise and she created financial independence for herself in the process... a miraculous 11th hour outcome. At the end of this run, she was honored with a retirement celebration. It was a 300+ person catered event. All spoke of her dedication, commitment, talent, and a multitude of other qualities that insured the success of the venture.

The culmination of the event was when they asked her to the stage for an impromptu speech. My mother spoke with grace, compassion, poise, and a deep sincerity that I hope someday to be able to embody. She inspired her peers and filled the room with hope. From her speech, "I was driven by a relentless persistence to succeed. I have always cared about people and I was devoted to my team and our success."

After living 50 years of my own life, my truest perspective on her life is that it was the way her life was meant to be lived. Care deeply about others and treat people with sincerity, use the correct fork at the dinner table, have a strong work ethic, use good grammar, work with integrity, buy a home, save money, never carry a credit balance, take care of yourself, and add value whenever you can.

I believe each life is a wonderful unfolding of the most interesting and intriguing story ever told. We should all be on the edge of our seats, present to this moment, just waiting for what comes next. My take-away... Love your life and all its circumstances, experiences, and content. It's short-sighted to believe that we understand why anything happens or what comes next.

Finding Stories on Your Hero's Journey

Terry Sprouse

"We must let go of the life we have planned, so as to accept the one that is waiting for us."
- Joseph Campbell

The Hero's Journey

In *The Hero with a Thousand Faces*, Joseph Campbell describes the Hero's Journey as a life-altering quest where, after passing through trials, the hero is transformed to a higher level of consciousness.

The stages of the journey are:
1) *The "call."* The hero sets off on a quest.
2) *The journey into unknown territory.*
3) *The supreme ordeal.* As Campbell puts it, "The cave you fear to enter holds the treasure you seek."
4) *Sharing the wisdom gained.*

Being on a Hero's Journey enhances the hero's perception. They feel like unseen forces are intervening to protect and guide them. The hero has a sense that everything happens for a reason.

The Hero's Journey of Abraham Lincoln

Abraham Lincoln had a belief that everything in his life happened for a reason.

After a loss to Stephen Douglas in the senatorial election of 1858, Abraham Lincoln slipped on a patch of ice in front of his house. His legs went out from under him, but he put out his arms as he fell, and caught himself before his body hit the ground.

"It was a slip but not a fall," he muttered. His face was lost in thought and he repeated, "A slip but not a fall." To Lincoln it was a sign that his quest to be president was not over. In fact, after publication of transcripts of the Lincoln-Douglas debates in newspapers, Lincoln became a household name all over the country.

Being on a Hero's Journey, we can convert the lessons we learn into stories.

Are the trials and tribulations of life good or bad? It may all depend upon how you look at it.

"The Big Picture"

Several years ago, when I worked in Honduras, I came across two stonecutters.

"What are you doing?" I asked the first stonecutter.

"Squaring the stone," the man replied.

"What are you doing?" I asked the second stonecutter.

"I am building a cathedral," the man replied.

Okay. The second guy was a little presumptuous, but he still gets points for seeing the big picture.

Your Hero's Journey

I believe that we are all on a Hero's Journey, and like Lincoln, we are endowed with the ability to discern the profound stories and parables that unfold before our eyes every day. We have only to be prepared to see them.

Convert Affliction to Anecdote

Are the catastrophes of life bad, or is life just trying to teach us a lesson? Let's look at a story as an example.

My mom was in and out of hospitals and rehabilitation clinics frequently the last couple of years of her life. It was a stressful time for both my mother and I. She often said, "My get up and go, got up and went."

Yet, even in the midst of this hurricane, there were also peaceful moments when we could chat while sharing lunch or when putting a jigsaw puzzle together. I admired how she responded to the difficulties with a kind nature.

However, my blood boiled when health care "professionals" treated her like an object rather than as a person. One doctor's assistant, in particular, habitually brushed off questions from my mother regarding health issues she was experiencing, with the attitude, "You won't be around much longer, just learn to live with you problems."

Yet, my mother never wavered in being thoughtful and accommodating both to him, as well as other nurses and doctors who sometimes seemed too busy to care. I often thought, "Shouldn't that be a priority for them?" Of course, there were also many health care workers, who extended kindness and understanding to my mother.

A humorous incident occurred in my mother's hospital room. My mom was in her hospital bed and a lady walked into the room and stared intently into my mother's eyes.

"Lois, how are you feeling? Why haven't you called? We have all been worried sick about you."

My mother and I both looked at her with blank expressions on our faces.

"Don't you recognize me, Its Bernice."

"I don't think I know you," said Mom.

Bernice looked at me and said, "Tell her who I am."

"I've never seen you before."

Then, this perplexed (and perplexing) woman suddenly walked back out of the room.

"Quick, lock the door. She might come back," Mom said.

Though most of her other body parts were worn out, Mom's funny bone was still working like new.

The Lesson

Her refusal to not let life's indignations tarnish her heart was not lost on me. She just smiled, joked, and kept on doing the best she could.

The lesson is not: She unjustly suffered and life is unfair.

The lesson is: By her living example, she showed me how to face life's final challenge.

As Dr. Seuss said, "Don't cry because it's over. Smile because it happened."

The Hero's Perspective

Are you squaring stones or are you building a cathedral?

You show me someone who is on a Hero's Journey and I'll show you a resilient, unflinching individual who converts life's challenges into stories of inspiration, strength and humor.

To paraphrase author Norman Maclean, from *A River Runs Through It*,

"In the end, all our failures and successes merge into one, and *a story runs through it.*"

Henry Ford - Keys to Success
David Smith

    Henry Ford's ability to focus enabled him to concentrate and achieve great success as the world's first mass producer of automobiles. This singular trait led him to eliminate distraction and create cars his way, ultimately through his Ford Motor Company. His focus was borne from a fascination with machinery, a conviction that excess must be eliminated, and a distaste for imperfection. Of the keys that enabled his success, two seem to stand out:

1) An intense and boundless curiosity (generally about mechanical things, and specifically about what was needed to create a horseless carriage); and

2) The ability to pull friends into his orbit and involve them in what he was doing.

    Henry was not the first to build an automobile. Others had created vehicles, had sold them (albeit in small numbers), and had patented various parts. But Henry's boundless belief in a better creation and his concentration on the next step, and the next, kept him focused on his objective.

    Born to a farming family in Dearborn, Michigan, Henry hated farming. He detested milk, never acquired a fondness for horses, and avoided the work associated with crops. When asked to work around the farm, he would show up, but frequently after a short period disappeared, never to be seen again that day. (If you have children who possess Houdini's disappearing act, take heart).

Curiosity

Henry did, however, enjoy figuring out how things were built, and by focusing his attention he learned a great deal from disassembling and reassembling mechanical things. His focus was not impeded by the unknown; in fact, the unknown seemed to drive him. At an early age, one of his father's hired hands opened the back of his watch and gave Henry a peek at its inner workings. His fascination led him to create his own tools from discarded items, and then to open and repair watches and other mechanical things. He fashioned small screwdrivers by pounding flat the ends of his mother's sewing needles. Birthday and Christmas gifts were fair game: Henry became adept at taking them apart to reveal their inner secrets, and then he put them back together. He could concentrate long hours and push through to figure out the unknown. When he needed a new tool to aid him he built that as well.

Henry was highly observant and watched for opportunities to learn. Shortly after his mother died, his father took 13-year-old Henry on a ride to Detroit, where they chanced upon two men operating the first non-horse-drawn vehicle Henry had ever seen. It was a steam-powered converted horse cart that was used for threshing. The operator gladly showed Henry how the coal fire boiled the water; how the resulting steam pushed the pistons; and how a chain engaged with a propelling wheel to turn the rear wheels, while a separate belt drove the machinery. It was a heavy thing, and few people around knew how to operate or repair them. Of particular interest to Henry was how the engine could continue to run and disengage from the drivetrain to allow the whole vehicle to stop while the engine idled, and then re-engage when the operator wanted to continue; he had thus witnessed a method that much later he would improve upon to provide this critical feature for his automobiles.

Henry's first job was with the Edison Illuminating Company, as a maintenance worker. He built upon his earlier successes and quickly gained a reputation for fixing things, and was soon given a raise and promotion. It also gave him the ability to scavenge scraps he needed as he began tinkering to create a single cylinder piston: a piece of steel pipe here, a rod there. These items allowed him the base materials, at no cost, from which he could experiment and create. He used these to tinker in his off hours.

When he began to build the components that would use gasoline to propel an engine, he found that a mist produced a much larger explosion than did increasing amounts of gasoline. He cobbled together his first gasoline engine: its ignition source was a wire that was attached to his kitchen light socket with its other end affixed to the cylinder; when his wife squirted a bit of gasoline into the cylinder, Henry threw the light switch on, which ignited the gas, drove the piston, and threw the engine into life. With this concept figured out, he realized battery power would provide a mobile ignition source. He then designed a sparking mechanism using washers of mica. This was the first spark plug.

As historian Richard Snow wrote about the process:

> *The ignition was difficult. The transmission was difficult, finally evolving into a combination of belts and a chain drive to the rear wheels. Everything was difficult. But the work went forward* (Snow, Richard. 2013. *I Invented the Modern Age: The Rise of Henry Ford*. New York, NY: Scribner. Page 58.)

Thus curiosity, coupled with focus, was one of the keys to Henry Ford's success. It is wonderful to witness focused curiosity. I have seen it in my colleagues Jerry, Joe, Kaushik, Chris, Lincoln, Amy and Donna as we have worked through the years perfecting our software.

When they catch a vision of what our future customers want, the vision alone seems to propel them. This has been true since our early days, when the tools that were available to build new features were only marginally available. When a workflow engine (a software application that manages business process wasn't necessary to capture the market, Kaushik recognized the need, and built the early production version that we have since improved many times over. When document management was necessary in order to replace paper files for our customers, Joe worked late hours for weeks and got it done. When it was necessary to create whole new cases from an existing case with minimal clicks, Chris described the vision and Lincoln built first a prototype and then a production version. They did this with the kind of energy you can only get from focus and curiosity.

There are, however, limits to what one can accomplish alone. At an early age, Henry's infectious zeal for invention, and his curiosity, attracted others, and he learned that some wanted to share in his adventure.

Friends

In the dawning age of horseless carriages, with no market yet developed, building a car was a hobby that yielded no financial benefit. Most of us need money for our basic needs of clothing, food and shelter. The typical source of money is a job working for someone else. Henry was no different; he had a young family to provide for, and he worked hard. But his evenings and spare moments were reserved to focus on his creation ... and he did so with a cadre of friends.

Henry learned from an early age that others enjoyed his hobbies and would participate if he led them with his friendly guidance:

> *For many of these (projects) he recruited helpers who were glad to follow his directions. This gift of swiftly being able to establish a cordial, happily received dictatorship would stay with him all through the time of his greatest achievements. As (his sister) Margaret put it, "He had the ability of getting his brothers and his companions to work for him"* (Ibid, 17).

To his Bagley Avenue shed, where at 30 years old he began working in earnest on his horseless carriage, many people accompanied him. First was his neighbor, Felix Julien, with whom he shared the shed but who removed all his belongings so Henry would have more space to work. Other regulars were James Bishop, who worked with Henry at Edison; Charles B. King, who had invented a brake beam used in the railroad industry, and also was interested in creating an automobile; and Oliver Barthel, a young assistant to King.

Ford described himself as making a number of parts, but that normally meant that he supervised others, actually them do the actual work:

> *For the most part, other hands than his fitted the spokes to the wheel rims. "I never saw Mr. Ford make anything," said one of his Bagley*

Avenue helpers. "He was always doing the directing." And the helpers he found, first-rate engineers like King and Barthel, always took the directing gladly (Ibid, 49).

He seemed to regularly keep things light. From childhood through adulthood he enjoyed pranks - and perhaps this tendency was an endearing part of his magnetism. He once covered all the doorknobs in his house in butter; tumbled a dummy made of stuffed pants and a shirt down the stairs to startle guests; securely nailed a workman's work boot to the floor; rigged a needle to jab a coworker's rear end; and put wooden croutons in a buddy's salad. It doesn't seem these gags turned people off, as they stayed in his circle.

In my company, we must rely upon each other, because there is no one person who knows all of our software, its capabilities, or our market. Part of this is because our software is too intricate for any one person to understand. Part is because none of us has the time to play with every feature. And part is due to the varied and changing nature of our customers' businesses. Regardless, it is vastly more productive, and more fun, when we are working together. One of us can get things done in time; with two we can challenge each other's' assumptions, get a good gut check, or simply commiserate and feed off each other's encouragement.

The Message

Henry went on to create America's first great automobile company, and propelled America into a highly productive age of mass manufacturing. His focus and curiosity helped him solve a number of problems, not the least of which was creating a car when there was no manual, no instruction, few materials, and limited tools. He had to push through issue after issue that very likely left many skeletons on the road to creating a spectacular industry.

He did so supported by friends who enjoyed working under his happy dictatorship. His life's work suggests that if we focus, keep our minds open and curious, and stay engaged with like-minded friends, we can achieve wonderful results in our lifetimes too.

Success While Waiting

Darrell Parrish Bakeman

Do you believe in miracles? I do! I have been waiting for a miracle to occur for a long time. I have been praying for a financial miracle ever since my children were young and I was a single parent entrepreneur.

After a successful career as a college administrator and non-profit organization executive, I started a public relations and marketing business. Starting a new business is quite a challenge. However, rearing two small children and paying for private school education at the same time is even more difficult. So, the need for more money was ever present in my mind.

My first client was a state senator that was running for a congressional seat. This was the first time I had worked on a political campaign. I was hired to do fund raising. I did a great job. The candidate won and three years later he ran to be the mayor of Chicago. Once again, I was tapped to do fund raising but on a grander level. I was very politically connected and highly regarded. I was close to power and money. In the eyes of the world, I was successful and had a lot of recognition. But, I still had to work very hard for money!

I knew that my life could be better if I was married. But, I was too busy rearing my children and operating my business. Having a relationship was "out of the question." So, I just started praying for God to grant me the desire of my heart—that was to be married! But not just to anyone. My prayer was very specific. It went like this: *"God, will you please grant me the desire of my heart to be married to a man that I could look up to. He will be spiritually equally yoked with me; he will be financially secure and independent; he will adore, cherish and respect me and he would make it possible for me not to have to work so hard!"*

I know God answers prayers! After twenty-two years of being a single, divorced, mother of two, I got married. In fact, I married the man that hired me to work in my first political campaign. A year after we were married, my husband retired me from working, so that I could support him in his professional endeavors. He also moved me from my hometown, Chicago, where I had established myself professionally, to Tucson, Arizona.

We were into our third year of marriage when I learned that he had stage four cardiomyopathy. He knew, but I did not! Once I got involved, we immediately took steps to secure the best medical care and to commence steps for a heart transplant. Unfortunately, they found spots on his liver, which resulted in him not being placed on the transplant list. While the spots were not remarkable at the time, they ultimately led to his demise. So, after only five years of marriage - I found myself single again! In a town where I had no roots.

When my husband died, everything in my life changed! I recorded these words in my journal:

I have never experienced such emotional pain, separation and changes in relationships as I have this year and all at one time.
1. *My husband is dead!*
2. *The financial things that my husband put in place did not come to pass.*
3. *I am engaged in a law suit with the company my husband founded to honor contracts and to pay funds obligated to me.*

4. *My elderly father's problems became my problems.*
5. *I am estranged from my family because of my control of the family property in Mississippi.*
6. *My health is not the best. I have a skin problem; my hair is falling out and my liver has been compromised. All because of the stress of this year.*

I believe that the only way that I could deal with all of this was by the grace of God. I am a strong Christian that knows and lives by the "Word of God." The day the law suit was before the judicature, I was studying a Larry Burkett Biblical Finance course that required memorizing a Bible verse. The one for that day was, *"I know what it is to be in need, and I know what it is to have plenty. I have learned the secret of being content in any and every situation, whether well fed or hungry, whether living in plenty or in want. I can do all this through him who gives me strength"* (Phil.4:12-13).

After 13 months and a lot of money in legal fees, I settled for 17% of what I was entitled too. I knew it was time to move on! I believe all that was lost, will be restored. So, I am waiting for God to restore my finances! Once again, I am single! And, I am praying for a financial miracle!

I am a Godly woman! By that I mean that, "I trust the Lord with all my heart; and do not depend on my own understanding. I seek His will in all I do and therefore He shows me which path to take!" These words might seem familiar to you because they are a first-person paraphrase of Proverbs 3:5-6 from the Bible. I find them particularly appropriate as I write about success. You see for me, true success can only be measured by becoming the person God wants me to be and reaching the goals He has set for my life.

I have a reasonable retirement income and health insurance. However, I do not own the home I live in. I knew my investment money would eventually run out. My plan was always to generate money the way I had in the past—as a consultant or business owner.

The problem was that as I grew closer to God, it became more difficult for me to move forward on plans I hatch in my office. I had done that many time in my career with a decent amount of success. But, I just couldn't seem to move forward.

Despite incorporating the business, securing a web name, setting up a bank account, filing for trademarking of the name, writing prospectus for a business plan and even having business cards printed—I just couldn't move without knowing that this was the path that God intended for me. There were no open doors, no people of influence walking beside me, no promptings or words of knowledge giving me direction. I knew in my soul, that I was not committed to this business and more importantly, God was not either!

At the beginning of 2016, I read *Intentional Living: Choosing a Life That Matters* by John Maxwell. The theme of this book is that: **when you intentionally use your everyday life to bring about positive change in the lives of others, you begin to live a life that matters.** This statement had a major impact on me. I want this final chapter of my life to matter.

I have less life ahead of me than behind! If I am fortunate to live into my mid-nineties, like most of my paternal relatives, then I currently have less than 9,000 days! That does not seem like a lot of time. The reality of my projected number of days left on this earth made me shift my focus from finding ways to earn additional income to supplement my retirement, to being significant. According to Maxwell, "To be significant, all you must do is make a difference with others wherever you are, with whatever you have, day by day!"

I decided to do what was at hand. I do what I believe God is directing me to do using the talents and abilities that He has equipped me to use. So, I volunteer my services to people and organizations that needed my help. One such organization is *Bridge Prison Ministry*.

I became connected with *Bridge Prison Ministry* after meeting Pete and Sandy Quinonez, the founders. I was so impressed with these two people because they have been doing this ministry for ten years while working full time jobs.

The ministry founders and a group of dedicated volunteers from local churches go into prison units four days a week to teach a life skills course, to conduct regular church services, and to lead prayer and healing services for inmates, two years prior to their release. I am helping *Bridge Prison Ministry* transition from a ministry that serves a few, to becoming a non-profit service organization that can serve many.

God wants you to be successful. To be a true success means becoming the person God wants you to be and reaching the goals He has set for your life. To know what God wants you to do— you must know God!

Knowing God has very little to do with going to church and being a good person. Knowing God is just like knowing a person - you must have a relationship. Very simply, this means talking with God about your everyday life, not just what you need and when you want Him to do something! It means getting to know what He is all about - his character and his expectations. The Lord's guidance will become clearer as you read His Word, pray for direction, and seek godly counsel.

You do this by reading the Bible. If you have never read the Bible, I know how daunting this might sound. But in the age of electronic devices, it has become a lot easier. There are several Bible Apps that can get and keep you connected. I like "You Version" and "Thru the Word."

In addition to knowing God, you need to experience God! Thinking about God and knowing him intellectually is not enough. I know God because I know-He knows me. He shows up for me.

- He helped me rear, educate and provide for my children while I was a single parent
- He equipped me with skills, resources and opportunities to have a successful working career
- He blessed me with access, recognition and earthly success
- He answered my prayer to be married to exactly the type of man I desired
- He provides a steady source of income for my living expenses and health care needs
- He strengthens me as I navigate my finances during my retirement
- He blesses me, so that I can be a blessing to others

What I know for sure is that God will continue to bless and show up for me. I believe that God will answer my prayer for a financial miracle - because I know God and He knows me!

I leave you with one of my favorite Bible verses:

Psalm 37:3-7

"**Trust** *in the LORD and* **do good**;
you will live safely in the land and prosper.

Take **delight in the LORD,**
and **he will give you the desires of your heart.**

Commit everything you do to the LORD;
trust him *and he will* **help you:**

*He will make your righteous reward shine like the dawn,
your vindication (justice of your cause) will shine like the noonday sun.*

Be still *in the presence of the LORD,
and* **wait patiently** *for him to act;"*

So, to be successful God's way, trust, do good, delight, be still and wait patiently for your reward!

3
Special Moments

You must live in the present, launch yourself on every wave, find your eternity in each moment.

Henry David Thoreau

Man's Best Friend
John Grand

"A dog is the only thing on earth that loves you more than he loves himself." -- Josh Billings

For as long as I can remember, dogs have been a pleasant and serene part of my life. I have been fortunate to have dogs of many breeds to be my companions, some registered breeds, but a good many of the *Heinz 57* variety. All of them unique in their own personality and loyalty. All of them loved and appreciated, but a few stick out in my mind as having been very special.

First, there was Angel, a little brown Chihuahua who loved to ride in the car laying on the back of my seat wrapped around my neck.

Sonny, a golden cross between a Lab and a Shepard, liked to jump the backyard fence when he became amorous, and returned home with what seemed like a smile on his face. Fiercely loyal, he would stay by my side when we were out together. Once while swimming in a lake, I dove down to see just how deep the water was and when I disappeared, Sonny jumped into the water and came after me. Sonny swam deep underwater looking for me. I had never seen a dog swim underwater before. It was very special to me.

Another special companion was Lady, a black and white mixed breed that adopted my Army Company in Vietnam and rode on my the Armored Personnel Carrier (APC) whenever we went out on a mission. Lady was special and I believe saved many lives by her habit of jumping off the APC and running along the jungle trails to set off booby traps left by the Viet

Cong. Lady was wounded several times and put back together by the company medic each time. She seemed to look at all of us as her "pack" that she had to take care of. Lady had a brilliant instinct to find roadside bombs and an overabundance of loyalty that she shared with every member of my company. She was still active when I left the Company to return to the United States and although I tried to find out what happened to her, I was never able to track her after I left. I still think about her with a feeling of deep affection.

While living in Spain, I used to take morning runs at 5:00 AM. I ran along the highway and enjoyed the early morning breaking dawn. One morning I noticed a movement in the high weeds along the road and saw a small dog face looking out at me. I stopped and went over to see it, but it ducked back in the weeds and disappeared. I continued my run, but the next morning the face was back in the same place, looking at me again. I went to get a closer look and again it disappeared in the weeds. On the third morning he was again watching me from the weeds. I stopped and looked at him, but instead of moving closer to him, I continued my run. I made my normal turn and returned to my home. As I was unlocking the front gate, I heard a noise behind me and when I turned there was the dog, sitting and holding up one paw, as if to say "can I come in?" I opened the door, reached down and picked him up and took him into the house.

He was full of burs, and smelled pretty bad. I took him in to the bathroom and ran a bath, set him in the tub and started to remove the burs and noticed that he had several wounds, someone had shot him and left an open wound on his right side. On his left side were some teeth marks as if a larger animal tried to bite him. His tail had been cut off and, in short, he was a very pathetic looking creature. My heart went out to him and I decided that he would stay with me.

I called him "Tramp" and promptly took him to the local veterinarian for a check-up and shots. We found that his weakened health was due very bad tooth decay. After removing the bad teeth, his health improved and he became my constant companion around the small Spanish village we lived in.

On one occasion, I had to travel out of Spain and left Tramp with my neighbors to look after him. I was gone for a month and when I returned I went to the neighbor's house to pick up Tramp. He was asleep by the fire place, so I sat down to tell my neighbors about the trip. Tramp woke and groggily gazed at me. He finally recognized me and, as if being shot out of a canon, he leaped from the fire place to land on my lap. He licked my neck and snuggled as close as he could get to me. My neighbors said Tramp had tears in his eyes.

Unfortunately, Tramp still had the urges of a wild dog and no matter how much I fed him, he still tried to eat any food he found on our walks. When I was with him I could stop him, but one night I was working on a script for an English radio show I did for a Spanish radio station, and Tramp came to me letting me know he had to go out. As I was busy, I let him out into my yard, with walls on three sides and a closed gate. What I didn't realize was that Tramp was small enough to fit between the bars on the gate.

Tramp disappeared. I went to the radio station and announced that Tramp was missing and asked the radio audience for help in finding him. Tramp and I were pretty well known around the village. Weeks went by without any word on Tramp, until one day the gardener came to me and let me know that he found Tramp, under a stairwell several houses away from my house. Sadly, he was dead, apparently from eating poisoned food the night he disappeared. In those days, the area of Spain I lived in had a problem with packs of wild dogs. The local government spread poisoned meat products around the village to kill the dogs. Unfortunately, Tramp was one of them. I have never forgiven myself for letting him out alone.

On another occasion, while still in Spain, my wife and I went to see some newborn puppies at a friend's house. There were only two left, one male and one female. The female was a tiny little thing and had taken shelter under the lawn mower. When she looked out and saw us, she walked over to sit by the toe of my boot. She gazed at us with a lovely look in her eyes. In short, she adopted us on the spot. How could we say no? We took her home, such a small thing that I could hold her in the palm of my hand. On the way home, a song by Cyndi Lauper came on the radio and we decided to call her Cindy. She was a joy, learned fast and became a very obedient companion, and she was a joy to the entire neighborhood. Spanish children would come to our house and ask if they could play with Cindy. She was still very small, and I held my breath while they rode their bikes, holding Cindy in one hand, while steering their bikes with the other.

Cindy, as all the others, had her own personality. She let us know when she was pleased with our performance and when she wasn't. For example, one of the nightly TV shows we watched was *M.A.S.H*. We would be downstairs, with the TV on upstairs. As soon as Cindy heard the introduction music to *M.A.S.H* she would run upstairs, jump on the couch and lay on the towel we had placed there for her. We would come up and sit on the couch with her between us and watch the show. As soon as the show was over and the music came back on, Cindy would jump off the couch and run downstairs and get in her bed in the kitchen, as she knew it was time for us to go to bed.

However, when we went on vacation and left her with friends, she let us know she did not appreciate being farmed out. Upon our return, we fell back into our nightly routine, the only difference was that when Cindy heard the *M.A.S.H* music, she would run upstairs, but not get on the couch. Instead, she would lay between the couch and the TV and show us her rear-end for about a week before forgiving us and finally getting back on the couch between us. Cindy lived with us for 13 years and traveled around the world with us, from Spain to New York, to Arizona, over to Saudi Arabia and finally returned home to Arizona, before age caught up with her and she left us.

Yes, there were many dogs in my life, each one a charmer and each with a personality all their own. I will always reflect on the memorable times we shared together and remember them fondly.

A house without a dog is not a home.

Marching Band on the Street

Yontaek Choi

It is 5:00 am on Sunday morning. The street is almost empty, well, except for three cars. Two cars are driving side by side, at exactly 40 miles per hour, on the two lane street with a 40 miles per hour speed limit. There is a third car behind them. It is quite obvious that it wants to pass. It keeps speeding up and down, near and far behind them and it keeps changing lanes back and forth. But it can't pass because the two cars in front are blocking the road and won't let the third car pass. No, this is so wrong. There are only three cars in the entire block and there is a traffic jam!

"Anybody driving over the speed limit are jerks, anybody driving under the speed limit are losers, and anybody driving at the speed limit are morons." I was watching *CNN Headline News* and that's what the news anchor said. She just gave a big laugh out-loud and moved on, but does that statement reveal our feelings about other drivers on the street? We say things like that probably because we don't like those driving faster than us and those driving slower than us. At this point, I want to think about a pleasant way of driving. What do you think is the most important factor which will make our everyday driving experience safer and more pleasant?

We tend to think, "I am the driver driving at the right speed." Those driving slowly think they are correct because they drive slowly and those driving fast think they are correct because they drive fast. According to a 2012 survey by Allstate Insurance, 67% of the respondents rated themselves as "excellent" drivers, while the "excellent" driver rate for other people was only 22%. In other words, the majority of us think, "I am the good driver while others are the bad drivers," but the person driving next to you has exactly the same idea. Somebody must be wrong.

If you believe the speed limit sign of 40 mph means you must drive at 55 miles per hour and the sign number should be interpreted, not as the maximum speed but as the average speed, you may complain other drivers are wasting your time. However, if you have a sixteen year old son, what would be the two words that come to your mind automatically when you hand over a car key to him? Aren't they, "Don't Speed!"?

If you insist we must drive exactly at the speed limit, and if you are an extremely proud law-abiding citizen, you may point out other drivers and yell "Violators!" Let's suppose you were on Highway 93, the highway with a single lane in each direction between Phoenix and Las Vegas. During the entire 300 mile of driving, you set the cruise control at 65 mph because the speed limit says 65 mph, never checking the wing mirror and never looking back with the rear-view mirror at the long, long line of cars behind you. You just contently enjoy the moment, "What a beautiful day! How come there are no cars on the highway? Am I the only one going to Las Vegas today?" After the four and half hours of comfortable driving, you see the glittering lights of the city dazzling in front and sing a happy song, "I did it My Way." No! The road is not 'My Way,' it's not 'Your Way,' but it's 'Our Way.'

If you believe we must drive below the speed limit, even though that may sound like an insane idea, I can find many reasons why sometimes we drive very slowly. You may be a stranger in the city looking for a sign, there may be a new-born baby in the car, or a birthday cake may be sitting next to you and the name of the street you just turned onto happens to be Roller Coaster Road.

For these types of drivers, do you see sometimes they may want to drive at a different speed? I want to insist that there is not one correct speed which is always correct for every situation. My point is it's not the speed that matters. Then what is it?

My 16 year old son plays a *mellophone* for his school marching band. Whenever I watch their marching band performances, I feel amazed by the harmony they can create with a series of unrelated movements. They walk, sometimes slowly, sometimes fast and sometimes backward. They march. They run. They turn and stop. With a big finale of fanfare, they finish the performance and all the parents stand up, clap and shout, "Yeah!" We cheer for them because they have just demonstrated a harmonious orchestra of discipline and coordination by carefully following the footsteps of the next person and by keeping an eye on the signals of the drum major. I have watched hundreds of marching band performances on YouTube, but I have never seen any of them fall or bump into each other during the seemingly crazy and complicated performances.

I can only say, that's the power of coordination and respect, respect to the person next to you, in front of you and behind you. Drivers can also create the same harmonious experience, if we are able to respect the drivers next to us, and follow the light signals and regulations.

What matters is not how fast or how slowly we drive, but how considerate of other drivers and how respectful we can be for their intentions. If a car is moving fast or slow, probably there is a reason for that. If a car cuts in front of me, probably there is a reason for that. If you know your little child sitting next to you will drive exactly the same way as you do at the age of 16, you may think again when you feel like running yellow lights. If you have the compassion for the drivers behind you on a single lane highway and feel their frustration, you may want to turn off the cruise control.

    What we need is respect and consideration for other drivers in order to reduce anger, frustration and misbehavior on the street. It will make our everyday driving experience safer and more pleasant.

Viewing Life Through Poetry
Arthur G. Lohman

During my school years, neither English nor Literature were among my favorite subjects. Also, I was not impressed with my writing skills. Now, years later I have written over a hundred poems, some of which have been published or turned into songs.

I have also written and presented dozens of speeches, entered and won *Toastmasters* Area Humorous Speech Contests, placed 2nd in a *Toastmaster* Division Contest, and I have written two plays. *Dying To Join* was the second play that I wrote. It was written for the 90th anniversary of *Toastmasters International* and was performed at the *District 3 Toastmasters Conference* held in Tucson, Arizona. The *Toastmasters* in the play were from various parts of the state of Arizona. Rehearsals were almost non-existent. The actors read from their scripts during the performance. None of those in the play had the last scene. They were given it at the start of that scene. Needless to say they were as surprised at the end as the audience was. This may have been the first and only time a play was performed at a *Toastmasters* conference.

My latest poem, *Nil per os* (nothing through the mouth), was written two days before I went into surgery. I had been suffering extreme stomach cramps for about two days. Finally, I gave into the urging of Arlene, my life partner, to see a doctor. At 9:20 Monday night I walked into the emergency room at Saint Joseph Hospital, Tucson, Arizona. I thought I would be there a few hours and sent home after treatment and medication. But finding that I had an extremely high white blood count meant that I had a severe infection and needed treatment to deal with it right away. That night of the 21st of November 2016 I was admitted to the hospital. I did not know that my stay would last twenty days.

My Surgeon, Doctor Kashaf Sherafgan, had drawn us a picture of the approximate location of the small bowel obstruction. The exact location, as well as what caused it, was a mystery to her, as the CAT scan only revealed a sizable black spot in my bowels. When she got inside, she found that I had a perforated appendix along with a tumor. The appendix had become a mass of tissue which had adhered itself to my colon. I wound up getting a right *hemicolectomy* with *ileal resection*. In layman's terms, part of my colon was removed and the remaining colon section was attached to my intestines. The tumor and other tissue samples were sent for biopsy. Fortunately, the results showed they were benign. After twelve days of being fed through a tube, I was feeling somewhat "blue" and thought maybe I should write a poem to cheer myself up before my Sunday surgery.

Nil per os

"Good morning Mr. Lohman!" **Boomed** *me to semi-consciousness. Was God telling me I died of stomach cramps?*

"Did you have a bowel movement?" **Boomed** *the voice again. I must be alive, God, sounds like a doctor. Still somewhat asleep, I thought* ***I hope not!*** *I'm still in bed, not on the pot.*

Am I dreaming?

"Did you pass gas?" **Boomed** *the voice. Oh dear not only am I alive but I must be a hostage trapped in a hospital room.*

Why would I pass gas? I might need to save it and sell it later to ransom myself out of here.

After all cars run on anything these days. I only hope I can save enough of it.

*Suddenly a **MEGA QUAKE OF TEN PLUS MULTIPLE PAIN ERUPPTED FROM THE EPICENTER OF MY BOWELS,** rattled my brain to reality. I'm here because I can't pass gas. My dispenser is plugged!*

*Ooh! With this discomfort, I hope when I pass it. It will be, **HIGH TEST PREMIUM JP4 ROCKET ENGINE GAS, THAT WILL BLAST THIS BLOCKAGE TO OUTER SPACE!***

*Hold on, I'm not, **IRON MAN!** Oh well, back to the drawing board!*

I will admit that writing this poem and sharing it with the medical staff did help. Especially since, I did not realize how close my brush with death really was.

My next two poems deal with those who intend ill will to others. They will use whatever dogma is available to coerce, influence, or force others to follow lock step in carrying out their evil intentions. Recent events show that mass murder is one such tool they use.

Chattel

Slaughtered
   like cattle
      politics

ideology
perverted excuses

I wrote this poem long before ISIS rose its ugly head in Syria and Iraq. It was written after the 9/11 attacks on our soil that killed thousands of innocent men, women and children. We now have terrorist in dozens of countries killing thousands of innocent people each year.

Absent of Humanity

Consumed with rage
A diabolically
   clever
      creature
         evolves

There will always be critics in this country when we march our young people off to war. As a Vietnam Veteran I would not want my sons or anyone's child to needlessly fight in war just for the name of "war". War is not a game to be played. When we see the brutality being committed against innocent people, we do not help them or ourselves by just being witnesses to wrong doing and mass murder. When war becomes necessary to protect innocent life we need to fight it in all seriousness with as few casualties as possible. This next poem was written because no matter how well one is prepared to engage in war, the price is always high.

Stern Discipline

War
After learning lesson well
Teachers
Wrath

Still felt

    I was trying to find a poem to write and out of nowhere this one appeared. I was a member of the Utah Poetry Society at the time. I realized that we were all trying to express to others the truth we felt inside. Truth is not something to hide from others but to be shared with all.

Metered Honesty

Poets don't lie
They just-
manipulate
truth-
until it
rhymes

    I remember there was a time in my life that I thought I was on the right path in life. But one morning I realized how lost I was.

Nowhere

Wrong track
   Wrong station
      Didn't change over at my connection
         Just kept going and lost my direction

    It was that day, when I realized that I had to find my way back to the right path. How long this journey is I don't know.

Epiphany

Beyond Status Quo
Destiny lies

Against tide
I must swim
Or
Drown

Thinking about life and how it came about has always intrigued me. I wonder if others hold the same fascination about its origins. Human history shows how adaptable we unique creatures are. Able to survive in the most hostile of environments whether it be the terrain, weather, carnivorous animals, etc. Given the ability to use the various resources provided us by nature we have submerged to the depths of the oceans, to walking on the moon. My next two poems express my wonderment. *Chaos Theory*, teaches us to think outside the box of traditional science that seeks predictability of outcome. Chaos is the science of studying things that are impossible to predict or control, like turbulence, weather, or our state of mind. Many of the complex systems of this earth are by nature chaotic. Hence the title "Chaos Theory."

Chaos Theory

Man
Mother Nature's
Most prodigal
Child!

Did she know
What she did?

    Or

Too late

Found out.

This next poem shows that man is both capable of doing good for the world or bad. Specifically, on countless occasion mankind has rescued endangered species from extinction. We also establish governments for the betterment of all. Yet at the same time, so capable of behaving so hideously towards our fellow man.

To Be or Not

Man's creative mind
Power to
Crush
Or
Shape
Mold
His reason to be

I wrote this poem because I found out that I really could dance to the music of the 70's. Unfortunately, I had a difficult time conversing with the opposite sex. I did not know what to say other than, "Would you like to dance?" Dancing was my way of communicating to them how interested in them I was. Not being good at small talk I was hoping that they were interested enough in me. To start it off once we left the dance floor. But maybe they were as awkward as I was in in the art of small conversation. But as I have found out *since*, that being a good dancer was only part of the equation. Being able to hold a conversation was as important if not more so, than being a good dancer.

I was confident in my ability to entertain others with my style of dance. This also became an internal foundation to build my confidence in becoming both a poet and speaker. I wrote what I felt inside me, just as I used my dancing to express those same emotions. I would use my poems to build my speeches around and became better at conversing with both genders. I also felt more comfortable in sharing the poems I wrote outside the *"Hill Climbers" Toastmasters International Club* that I had joined in 1985 at Hill Air Force Base, Utah. Finding out what you are good at can be a springboard into improving other areas of your life that you are weak in. Since then I have also become an actor. I have now been on both stage and on film.

The Dancers

He loves to dance.
All night he sought
one woman
 who'd say yes.
Who would share his love.
All had said no.
Seeing a lone figure
sitting in the corner.

Their eyes meet.
She's the one!
With hand out reached
he asked, would you, like to dance?
In each others arms, they float
over the crowed floor.

Their love of music,
 letting it flow into their souls.

Disciplined bodies
 rhythmically synced,
moving in expression
of the melody within.
Two sprits harmonized as one.
No one gave them a chance.

Taking command of the floor.
They danced and danced.
All the others, sit in corners
"watching".

When I became a parent I realized that not only was I responsible for my wife and myself. But also for our two sons, who depended on both their mother and me, to help them through their early life.

Suspended Above

When a child in the dark night
On the grass in my backyard
I would lay
Eyes fixed on the twinkling
lights above
My mind traveled to and beyond the
stars suspended
In the endless universe stretched
above my backyard

After years of turmoil and
Heartbreak
Looking in the eyes of my son
I remembered my youthful dreams
of space travel

I wonder
will my son continue
to dream
Or years later like I
only remembering them
When gazing in the eyes of his son

    I felt the urge to write something even though this idea had not entered into my thought process. I had no paper with me to write on, I found this used envelope and carefully disassembled it where it was glued. Now I had a piece of paper I could write on. Why this thought came to mind I do not know. But perhaps this thought was in my heart and not in my mind.

This Tattered Envelope

How would she feel?
If she knew,
That on the inside of this torn, worn envelope,
My love for her I did write.
At our first meeting young at heart and love we were.
Now the years have past.
Tatters and tears wear upon our faces.
Will she now as then smile with glittering eyes.
Sighing at this romantic thought.
Will she peek inside this tattered torn envelope?
To see, a youthful thought.
Of how innocent and simple our love was.
Is it now?
If thrown in the wastebasket this tattered envelope goes.
With no idea of the hidden treasure that lies inside.
Or thought given, to an old man's, wishful thinking then a
once young maiden, now becomes old.

But if in the heart and mind of a still young maiden these words are cherished.
Then I have the answer I seek.

In my youth I used to be extremely self-conscious about being criticized by others. I was awkward in verbally defending myself from those who teased me. Now in my older years I am better able to use words to express myself as well as to use poetry to poke fun at others and myself.

Shampoo

It's not fair I'm losing my hair
It should be those of you who stare and glare
And some funny remark blare
Whose hair should wear!

Then maybe you would take care not tease me
about my head so bare.
When unkind words about my lack of hair are flying in the air.
I feel like hibernating like a bear.
Beware for in my lair I will dare.
To formulate a shampoo with ingredients rare,
That will take your head full of hair
And turn it so bare
That a bowling ball
Will not compare!

As I mentioned in an early poem I believe man is capable of both good and evil. It is how we use what we are given and the way we treat others that defines our motives.

Humans

Man was born
Unique he was
A strange looking creature
Never seen before
Given a brain to reason with
He devised new plans and ways to live
Tools he designed to suit his needs
Wheels to roll
Ships that float
Books to read
Telescopes to see beyond
Planes that zoom
Guns that shoot
Chemicals that kill
Bombs that radiate
And computers that one day
Might think like Man

I will end this chapter with the poem below. Before I do, I will mention that these poems are not written in chronological order. The reasons are that some poems lead to another or events of the day that strike me personally. Regardless of where in the world they occur. On the morning of June 14th, 2017, *United States Representative* Steve Scalise was shot. If it was because he was a *Republican* congressman, it reinforces why I am sharing my poetry. We already have movements in this country that pits American against American.

Political, climate change, religious or other ideologies are prompting both vitriolic language and in some cases mob violence. I do not want violence for one excuse or another, becoming commonplace. Violence should never replace the use of civil dialogue to air our different points of view, from occurring, in this great country. I want people to think for themselves and question any groupthink that I see growing and growing in this country today. I cannot fully explain why I started writing poetry and as such I will close with this poem.

Gift of Words

Someone asked why don't you write a poem about God?
You have a way with words.
So I wrote a poem about Him.

At first I thought it easy.
For I have a way with words.

This time they just didn't come to mind.
Were the words having their way with me?
Was God reciting a poem for me.
And I didn't want to listen to or use His words.

My poem about Him was my poem not His.
My words were mine, not His.

After finishing my poem with great difficulty.
I was going to recite it to my friend.

No words, could I speak!
My words might be mine, but my voice was His!

I still write poems about Him.
But I listen to His words.
My poems about Him are His not mine.

I have learned, if I refuse His gift of words.
I refuse His gift of voice.

Disobedience Pays Off

Philip Schultz

January 20th, 1945.

On my 24th mission, over Linz, Austria, an anti-aircraft bomb went off under the nose of our B-24 Bomber. One piece cut the windshield in front of my face but did not break through. Another piece went through the navigator's compartment. It missed the navigator, but severed the trim tab control cable under my feet.

The plane went into a roll to the right which our pilot, Captain Irving Abravaya, had difficulty controlling. He called the lead plane and said we were bailing out. He punched me on my left shoulder, and yelled,

"Bail out Oscar (my nickname in combat), I can't bail out until you bail out!"

I unbuckled my seat belts that went around my waist and over my shoulders, fastened my chest parachute pack, and pulled the knob on my seat which had a cast iron shield around my head and back. This allowed my seat to roll back, and I stepped out into the open 20 foot long bomb bay onto a foot wide ramp with open air on either side.

Half of the 10 man crew stared at me from the front bulkhead and the other half from the rear bulkhead to see what I was going to do. I looked around me and saw fluid leaking out of a reservoir. I took a handkerchief and plugged it up.

I looked down at snow-covered Austria and realized that if I bailed out first and the others did not bail out immediately, I would find myself alone in a foot of snow in one of the coldest winters on record. I would likely freeze to death or be made a prisoner of war.

I looked at the cockpit and at my eye level saw the autopilot control with nine adjustment buttons on it. I threw it in. The plane lurched. The pilot, still in the left pilot seat, turned it off. Still in the bomb bay, I threw it back in and adjusted it. The plane leveled out and seemed to be under control. I returned to the copilot's seat. No longer in formation, we flew back to *San Giovanni Air Field*, Italy, by ourselves. We landed using the autopilot instead of the usual manually controlled landing.

Back on base, we had our usual shot of whiskey to calm our nerves, then went in for debriefing. The pilot had gone in ahead of me and the top turret operator, who was in the room with him, heard the wing general say to Abravaya,

"I hear your crew doesn't obey you. Put your copilot in for a DFC (Distinguished Flying Cross) for saving the crew and the airplane."

A few days later, I was being tested to be rated pilot with Captain Abravaya in the copilot's seat as the test pilot. He simulated an 'engine out' by pulling the mixture control on the number one engine. This caused the super charger to stop suddenly and blew blades out, which cut the control cable to flight controls at the rear of the airplane. The plane went in to a dive. I tried the trim tab -- nothing happened. I said to myself,

"Boy, he's really testing me!"

I put my feet up on the glass covered instrument panel and pulled my control column with all my might. Abravaya looked over and saw what was going on and also put his feet up on the control panel. The two of us pulled the plane out of the dive. Then I thought again of the automatic pilot, threw it on, and was able to fly the plane back and land, using the auto pilot. It had saved us again.

I became a pilot and from then on, checked out new crews.

Footnote: The Distinguished Flying Cross ranks number 6 out of 106 military medals.

4

Live Your Dream

Certain things catch your eye, but pursue only those that capture the heart.

Ancient Indian Proverb

Why Do I Still Teach?

Myrna P. Fileccia

In job interviews, I was often asked the question, "Why did you decide to be a teacher?" In reality, it was teaching that found me, and not the other way around. When I was a young girl growing up in the Philippines, I dreamed of becoming a nurse, dressed in a white uniform and wearing a cap. In the 1960's, there was huge demand for nurses abroad. To go abroad was everyone's paramount dream. I was no exception. Unfortunately, nursing was way beyond the financial reach of my parents.

So, I became a teacher, just like my father and almost every aunt and cousin in the family. The Teacher's College (called Normal School) was the only school that my parents could afford to send me to. They advised me to earn a living as a teacher and to pursue my goal to be a nurse later, when I had more money. However, my future did not pan out that way. I graduated with a four-year degree in elementary education, and never studied nursing. Instead, I went on to earn advanced degrees in the field of Education.

Along the way, I discovered I was tailor made to be a teacher. I have an innate desire to motivate students to learn, and I experience a great joy when children respond positively to my teaching. There is nothing more gratifying than reading a picture book to children and to see their faces light up as they experience the wonder and pleasure of reading. I enjoyed the feel of energy and enthusiasm from my students as they would jump to their feet when I told them to "Get up and go!" I shared the children's excitement as they learned to play the recorder to the tune of "Twinkle! Twinkle! Little Star." As the children matured, they learned to say. " No, thanks, it tastes different," instead of saying, "Yucky," when tasting a new food. When studying patterns, it was amazing to hear them correctly say "red" at the right time in a "red-yellow-red-yellow" pattern, after only one example.

At 67 years old and still teaching full-time, I have become more laid-back, more patient and more understanding of young children. Yet, teaching has not always been this gratifying for me. It was especially stressful when I taught children in inner city schools located in dangerous areas of town. As a graduate student at *Columbia University Teachers College*, I explored diverse settings, to fulfill the requirements of my master's degree.

My baptism of fire was in a first grade classroom in a Catholic school in the Bronx area of New York City. The school placed a tremendous emphasis on keeping students quiet and orderly, not a simple task. At the end of each exhausting day, I breathed a deep sigh of relief.

At an independent school in Harlem, I struggled to keep the attention of 12 surly children. They much preferred to kick each other's feet under the table, than listen to me. It was a tough setting, but I developed some valuable teaching tools. Merely saying, "Don't make me use my 'teacher voice'!" did not seem to faze them. As a frail-looking Asian teacher amidst students twice my size, it was a blessing to have survived a year in a setting where drug vials were very much a part of the surroundings.

My degree in early childhood education landed me a Kindergarten job, and eventually the Educational Director's position in an international school in Manhattan, where I taught for nine years. Then, my career snowballed as I subsequently took teaching positions in Delaware, Connecticut, Arizona and Nevada. Teaching was my bread and butter. My goal was to keep doing this job that I not only loved, but also paid the bills. I was dedicated and hardworking. Winning "Teacher of the Year" and "Most Outstanding Professional" awards showed that I had the personality, professionalism and passion for teaching. Yet, there was still something missing.

When I turned 62 years old, I decided to take an early retirement from teaching to become a psychosocial rehabilitator. I worked with at-risk children in foster homes. Soon enough, working with troubled children took its toll, and the stress of dealing with violence on a daily basis became too much for me. You win some, you lose some.

Once a teacher, always a teacher. While in retirement, I sought volunteer opportunities to teach. Soon, I was hired as a teacher in a Christian School in Las Vegas, Nevada. Five years later, I moved to Tucson, Arizona. After a year of pursuing my passion for public speaking in *Toastmasters* (no, we do not sell toasters), I discovered I had a gnawing need to get back to the classroom again. I felt revitalized to return to my first love, but in a different setting. This time, in a daycare venue, with a small staff teaching DES (Department of Economic Security) subsidized students. They became the beneficiaries of my desire to rekindle my teaching career.

For the first time in my career, I was teaching not because I needed to, but because I wanted to. This unruly group of children needed structure and academic stimulation, but hardly a week went by without a few children being suspended and disenrolled. I was almost driven to walk out when in a contest of wills, an angry child spat on my face. After sincere apologies from his family, I decided to give it another try and I turned the unfortunate event into an opportunity.

Clearly, kids with behavior issues and learning disabilities desperately needed innovative teaching strategies to keep them engaged. My creative juices kept flowing, turning my classroom into an oasis of ideas. I caught the discerning eye of my director who was profuse with appreciation for my classroom activities. It felt great to assume the role of a teacher-mentor on lesson planning, classroom management and teaching techniques. And this was at a time in my career when I enjoyed "just" being a classroom teacher.

As we explored different themes, the children connected to my use of changing settings and virtual field trips to the farm, beach, and the carnival. The class once put on a puppet show adapted from *The Very Busy Spider*. They also participated in a fashion showcase of their own tie-dye shirts. In a matter of two months, the once rowdy children became a class of eager learners.

My defining moment came when my teacher assistant spontaneously asked me, "How did you discover that your mission in life was to be a teacher?" She was considering studying Education at the university. She said to me, "I feel lucky to be working with a passionate teacher."

Finally! This was the moment that I had long waited for. She caught me off-guard, I asked for some time to reflect on my answer. My reflection took me to a deep soul searching as to what is my purpose in teaching; what is most meaningful to me and the greatest joy I derive from it. This process was the most challenging research work in my life. Throughout my career, I never really articulated this essential belief about why I decided to become a teacher.

I believe my mission is to make a difference in the lives of young children. It makes me happy when a light bulb goes on over the head of a student, as they connect to something I am teaching in class. I got a lump in my throat when my Swahili-speaking student showed me a page from a book and said, "Rainbow," her first word spoken in English. Likewise, it tugs at my heart strings to watch a co-teacher instructing dance movement to the toddlers and see it "click" with them as they change from floundering bumpkins to delightful whales. Yes! They are learning!

I feel warm and tingly knowing that my employer fully supports my teaching techniques and my curriculum decisions, in line with developmentally- appropriate practices.

I have reached a point in my career where the joy of teaching is the reward in itself. I am changing the world one day at a time. I can say I have found my purpose in life, as a teacher.

My Toastmasters Journey

Randy Casarez

I will never forget the day. It was January 9, 1990 and I was 9-years-old. I remember sitting in the Principal's office wondering what I had done wrong. Suddenly, my mom, the school counselor, and the principal, all walked in. I knew at that moment, I was in trouble.

"What did I do wrong?" I kept asking myself.

I remember my mom looking at me with that motherly look. I was waiting for her to say something.

"Randy we wanted to let you know that we did some testing on you, and we have discovered that you have a learning disability" the school counselor, Mrs. Cain, said.

"Is this a good thing or is it bad thing?" I thought to myself. Honestly, I did not know what to think at that moment.

"Randy, I'm sorry, but we are going to have to put you in Special Education classes," she said.

At that moment, all I could remember was my head dropping. This was not good at all. This meant for the rest of my life I would be stuck in Special Education classes.

Many thoughts went through my head. For a moment, I did think about suicide, but something inside told me that I would be okay if I could only find my passion.

I could not describe the feeling, but I just remember thinking, "Everything is going to be okay."

Every year, I kept hoping to find my passion, but I could not find it. In middle school I thought my passion was basketball, but it wasn't. In high school, I thought that my passion was the Future Farmers of America (FFA), but like basketball, the passion died quickly. In my 20's. I thought my passion was being an actor, but it was clear that I was not any good. Acting was great at first, but it soon became boring. Playing other people just felt like I was hiding something.

I remember turning 30-years-old, and I should have been happy because I was about to get my Master's Degree in Accounting. However, I felt that even though I was about to be an accountant that this was not my passion. Writing had always sparked an interest in me, and I decided that I was going to try writing.

At the time I was into watching politics on CNN and I decided to write a short story about President George W. Bush. I wrote a fictional book called *The Big Ones* about how the main character, Jimmy Lopez, sends his girlfriend to Washington as an intern, and she ends up sleeping with President Bush.

Writing the short story was a great experience, but I would be lying if I said it was easy. It was a struggle. Even though I loved writing the short story, I was not good at it. Many of my friends will tell you that I'm not a good writer. It used to upset me, but the truth is that I'm not a good writer. I make a lot of grammar mistakes. For me it has always been a struggle to put my thoughts on paper.

Although I was 30-years-old, I was going through mid-life crisis. What was I going to do if I could not find my passion? How in the world was I going to survive?

One night I was talking to my older brother. My brother never has a problem giving advice.

"Randy, you should go to *Toastmasters*," he said

"What is *Toastmasters* about?" I asked.

"Randy, trust me, go to *Toastmasters* and it will help you network."

"I have nothing to lose and everything to gain," I thought to myself.

I remember the first time I walked into a *Toastmasters* club called *TV Toastmasters Live*. I loved the idea on being on TV. At that moment, seeing these Toastmasters speak so eloquently was amazing.

"This is a great opportunity to speak and to be on TV," I thought.

I wanted to become a member that night, but I met a member named Mark Salcido who was very encouraging.

"Randy you should come to my home club *Saguaro Toastmasters* he said. They meet every Monday night at the *Tucson City Council Ward Six* office."

Most people would have said "no" or "maybe." However, I was so excited that I said "YES!"

The following Monday, I was at the *Ward Six* office, and when I saw a full *Toastmaster* meeting, I was hooked. It was amazing at every meeting. I always had a chance to speak and have fun. I was even amazed that you could win awards at each meeting. The more meetings I went to as a guest, the more I realized I had found my passion.

I love to speak.

There is no better feeling in the world than giving a speech. Since 2011, I have given thousands of speeches. Although I have never been paid, I enjoy giving speeches. I feel the need to speak as often as possible. I have competed in Humorous Speech, International Speech, Tall Tales, Evaluation, and Table Topic Contests. I have won some and I have lost some, but I always enjoy competing.

There is no better feeling than motivating others through a speech. I still have people that come up to me, and tell me that they remember a speech that I gave two years ago. For the first time in my life, I feel that I can overcome any problem and be okay. Toastmasters has allowed me to look at things from a positive outlook on life.

It took me years to find my first accounting job, but because of *Toastmasters* I was able to get my first accounting job working at *Quick Associates*. *Toastmasters* gave me the confidence to interview well, and to land the job. *Toastmasters* has given me the confidence to write a novel, and soon I am going to self-publish my first book.

I'm excited about life, although I'm not rich and famous.

I have found my passion.

Every day I have to live with my learning disability, but every day I realize that I can be a success because I have found my passion to speak. No matter how many times I speak, I still find myself wanting to speak more. I never tire of speaking. Whether it is in *Toastmasters* or at any other type of special event, I am always going to want to speak.

I believe that the key to happiness is finding your passion.

From Woes to Wins with Three Action Types

Raleigh Ormerod

Are you facing an impossible situation? Take heart! I can show you how to turn it around.

I failed miserably as my peers prospered. I was too embarrassed to face them. Yet, I turned it around and arose as a leader. I learned behaviors that others can replicate with coaching and mentorship. Bestselling business authors have articulated the principles that I bring together for you here.

How did it come to this?

Sunday, February 14, 1988. My situation was dire. With a cry out to God and the universe, I demanded to know what I'd done to deserve such a fall from grace. The answer coming back to me was, *"IT'S COMPLICATED."*

I was 22, broke and heartbroken. My career and love life had failed to launch. I was living alone, paying off student loans plus apartment rent by working multiple low-paying jobs. My girlfriend had just left me. She was off cavorting with another guy, and I could do nothing but cry.

Isolated from family and friends, I'd been kicked out of my parent's home because of ideological differences among the various family factions and my choice of alliance within them. My 'beloved' status in the family disintegrated. *T'WAS COMPLICATED INDEED.*

Raleigh's 'list of woes' was complete:

- ✓ Career – failed to launch
- ✓ Romance – heartbroken
- ✓ Finances – very poor
- ✓ Physical Health – sleep deprived
- ✓ Mental Health – questionable
- ✓ Social/family relationships – damaged
- ✓ Need to change situation – desperate
- ✓ Knowing how to change situation – clueless

Glimpse a much better future

Fast-forward to my 10-year college reunion in October 1997. I was accomplished in an exciting career. I had created a whole new category of business and was in the process of launching a second major product line in another business category - each to become a famous billion-dollar brand. I'd won the lottery of love by marrying my college sweetheart. I was living in an avant-garde community with an enlarged circle of friends and family and owned multiple rapidly appreciating assets.

To ascend from devastating failure, I discovered and executed three specific types of action *that were completely within my control*. Significant improvement occurred within 3 months.

Allow me to build my case for your success. Then you can see and decide how it can work for you.

ACTION TYPE ONE: HARNESS NATURAL FORCES ALREADY PRESENT.

So why not simply call on God or anyone to bail me out? *It's complicated.* I never had much luck any time I'd asked God to change another person's behavior so that things would go my way. What if somehow the answers were already present?

No one is coming to save you, but someone is watching

Fear had blinded me to the greater reality, triggering a primal urge to flee or to fight or (in my case) *to hide*. It gets very dark when you stick your head where the sun doesn't shine.

Facing my fears of rejection and failure, it became clear that no one was coming to "save" me, but that 'Someone' was watching. Others facing profound crises had come to a similar conclusion. The "No one is coming, but someone is watching" insight is articulated by Darby Checketts (*Leverage: How to Create Your Own "Tipping Points" in Business and in Life*) in his account of the life of Ray Charles. The quest to understand who was watching over-rode the hopelessness.

Discover natural power sources

My martial arts instructor advises, "When you are attacked, look around immediately for anything that can be used as a weapon." This advice applies to all manner of troubles. Robert Cialdini (*Influence: The Psychology of Persuasion*) articulates the insight: all that's needed to influence, change, and exert influence over a situation is to identify and leverage natural (but perhaps hidden) sources of power that already exist in the environment.

Sunday, February 15, 1988. I possessed almost no tangible assets except an old black & white TV that showed the 1988 Winter Olympics broadcast from Canada. I loved the Olympics. I had been a high school and college athlete. I had lived "the thrill of victory" and now I knew "the agony of defeat" – the TV station's Olympic motto.

Natural forces lay dormant. Raised on a farm, I had a work ethic but little financial means. I had financed a college degree mostly on scholarship. I was active in the student government and played NCAA Division III college football. Football taught me to use the other players and field geometry to create more options for my team. My fighting spirit, a powerful internal force, was re-awakening.

Step back to leap forward

Monday, February 29, 1988. Ironically, leap year 1988 gifted me one extra day to get my act together. I struck a lower rent deal with a *McDonald's Restaurant* co-worker. I gained a more affordable place to live and a non-judgmental buddy. He got me a better third-shift job delivering doughnuts in the peaceful pre-dawn hours.

Saturday, April 2, 1988. At the funeral of my beloved great grandmother, I reconnected with my Canadian relatives. Demonstrating genuine empathy, they asked me who, what, when, where, and why questions that clarified my situation. Someone was watching.

My cousin in medical school wanted to know what happened to my science career. I told Lori I didn't want to be a lab nerd and that I'd seen too much blood and guts growing up on the farm to be craving medical school. I believed my physical sciences degree prepared me for nothing else.

Lori redirected my thinking. She replied, "My brother went to engineering school and took business classes to create more career options. The engineering program at *Queen's University* is very good. Why don't you come to Queen's?"

ACTION TYPE TWO: CHOOSE THE MOST POWERFUL INTERPRETATION

Engineers greatly outnumber scientists in the workforce, but I had thought the rarity of scientists made them more desirable. I found a more powerful interpretation of the data. The economy could support more engineers. Engineers are more marketable, so engineers have more options.

Build your options

When you find yourself in a hole, *stop digging* immediately. I took a deep breath, turned my head upwards, and created more options. I had acquired engineering experience during a paid summer internship at a top school in Materials Science and Engineering. During my internship, the *University of Wisconsin* had arranged a full ride offer. "Don't go home," they said. "You don't need to finish your bachelor's degree - just stay here for a PhD!"

Considering present circumstances, I regretted having said no. Now, I chose the more powerful interpretation, one that would allow me to move forward. I recognized I had actual engineering experience and enough talent that world-renowned experts wanted me.

Friday, May 13, 1988. The *University of Minnesota* Materials Science program was rated #1, so I paid the department a visit. I returned from that visit with a summer research job and I was asked to apply to the graduate engineering program.

I generated a list of 17 graduate engineering programs. Renaming my 'List of Woes' to 'What Counts' Factors, I built a bigger, better playbook by supplementing choices others offered with options generated from my own research.

Raleigh's "What Counts' Factors:

- Career
- Romance
- Finances
- Physical Health
- Mental Health
- Family Relationships
- Use Current Education
- Cost to Change

Build and rebuild relationships

Keith Ferrazzi (*Who's Got Your Back?*) espouses a mindset of vulnerability to build strong relationships. I spent two college summers helping my grandparents remodel, rebuild, and maintain their home. They had paid me for services and provided room, board, and nurturing kindness. I asked for a similar arrangement to plan my next move.

The University of Minnesota offer materialized. So did Queen's and a few others. I chose Queen's because it provided the most options including international exposure.

Accept unexpected help

My grandparents noticed my squinting, so they got me prescription eyeglasses. That explained why I had been dropping the football and accumulating penalties my senior year. They hated to see me go, but extended their blessing to forge my own path. My grandfather even drove me 1000 miles to *Queen's University* in Canada. I could do nothing but acknowledge their unexpected gifts.

I got more unexpected help. I had previously returned from my Wisconsin internship for my senior year at *St. Olaf College* with growing physical anxiety. Now in Canada with free health care coverage, I went to the doctor who discovered a thyroid tumor that required immediate surgery. The growth, likely caused by radiation exposure during the Wisconsin material science internship, had temporarily disrupted my hormones. No wonder I did not feel quite right after working there. Thankfully, they caught it before it became malignant. The surgery was successful and left me without a medical bill.

ACTION TYPE THREE: EVOLVE FROM WOEFUL TO WINSOME WITH FOCUS CHARISMA

February 14, 1989. What a difference a year makes! I awoke on that Valentine's Day looking forward to a date that evening. I loved the Masters of Chemical Engineering program at Queen's, which was packed with marvelous mentors and charismatic cohorts. I was approached to run for the graduate student government. Upon graduation, my success in student leadership helped land the dream job with *Procter & Gamble,* a position that 500 other graduating Queen's students applied for.

Focus first on others

One key to radiating enchanting charisma is to focus completely on others. Olivia Fox Cabane (*The Charisma Myth*) describes this as *focus charisma*. The key to building good relationships fast is to make resolving the other party's social tension your primary concern.

In student government, I led with generosity. In reciprocation, many volunteers fully staffed my many committees. I recall returning from surgical recovery to be greeted by dozens of my new friends who were invested in the outcome, and my well-being. Leading with generosity is another critical mindset espoused by Keith Ferrazzi (*Who's Got Your Back?*).

Seek first to understand your customers, colleagues, and competitors

At *Procter & Gamble* (P&G) I led global cross-functional teams that developed and launched new products. In 1993, I accepted a promotion and transfer with my wife to Cincinnati where P&G had their world headquarters.

Like many P&Gers, I read Steven Covey (*Seven Habits of Highly Effective People*). One of my favorite chapters was, "Seek First to Understand." I initiated a deep in-situ dive into habits and practices of floor cleaning to ascertain why our cleaning products performed so well in the lab yet so poorly in the market. We developed a new consumer behavior model and a different set of product requirements for a more ideal cleaning solution. I became known as "The Father of the Mop," a champion for P&G's *Swiffer* that became a billion dollar brand. *Swiffer* happened because I listened with empathy to the exact language that market participants used to describe their pain.

When recruited to *Colgate-Palmolive*, I participated in the launch of *Colgate Total Toothpaste* with a sophisticated and very effective multi-channel marketing and advertising effort. This new product stole the #1 leadership share position from P&G's *Crest*. I got this wonderful opportunity based on the recommendation of a former P&G supervisor. Relationships matter.

APPLYING THE THREE ACTION TYPES

I've also applied these principles to launch companies and grow businesses - leading, advising, coaching and mentoring *Fortune 500* companies, startup companies, and community leaders.

As no one is coming to save you, stop digging. Consider sources of dormant but available power. Find people who challenge beliefs that hold you back. Let others contribute to your success. Create a larger playbook of options. Resolve the social tension of others.

When your world goes dark, you must carry the light in your heart. Not only for yourself, but also to become a known and present power for others.

License to Thrill

James Babcock
(Transcribed and rewritten by Rich Konkle)

So I should write something about being an entrepreneur? Er...okay here goes...

Well, I DO run my own, one-man business of freelance cartoonist and illustrator. Technically, I AM an entrepreneur. And even if I haven't "set the world on fire" with my success, I've stayed afloat, met a lot of great people, and worked on a variety of interesting projects --all while doing the thing I love.

What do you do if you want to be an entrepreneur?

Small-business courses --and I feel like I've taken a zillion of them-- will warn you not to rush into it headlong. Before you become the proverbial "bull in a china shop," you're supposed to step back and 1) ASSESS what you'll need...and 2) SELF-ASSESS what YOU bring to the table. To do this --I've been told repeatedly-- you use the acronym "S.W.O.T."

S.W.O.T. stands for "STRENGTHS" (what are your strengths?) ..."WEAKNESSES" (what are your weaknesses?) ..."OPPORTUNITIES" (does the market have a place for your prospective business?) ... and "THREATS" (what could kill your newborn business!).

A good enough acronym, I suppose. I'm not trying to swat S.W.O.T.

If you're planning a "conventional" business, S.W.O.T. is fine...but it's not much use for a freelance artist. The fact is, it just worried me to death! How can an artist measure his "strengths and weaknesses?" Art is subjective! And how do I plug-in data and metrics to assess the "opportunities and threats" of the cartoon art marketplace? I just want to draw comics and caricatures!

Yes, "freelance cartoonist and illustrator" is a strange, "none-of-the-above" kind of profession. It's uneven work with a nebulous and extremely scattered customer base. You have to hustle, network and self-promote like mad just to be seen and remembered. And the customers rarely seek you out.

Unlike plumbers or auto mechanics, nobody ever has "an art emergency." Nobody has ever said "Good Lord! We need a four-panel cartoon strip and six caricatures RIGHT NOW!"

"Sigh" - This is the life I've chosen.

In the words of *Super-Chicken*, "You knew the job was dangerous when you took it, Fred!"

...And just to make things really challenging, I've got a couple of other things to throw into the mix.

I've had Schizoid Effective Disorder my entire adult life...and a case of Dyslexia, which went undiagnosed throughout my childhood...and have I mentioned my prolonged bouts of Depression, many years ago? I'd say these would go in the "WEAKNESSES" category of S.W.O.T., wouldn't you?

In our current culture of victimhood, it would be easy to "accept" my mental health issues and learning disability, give in to depression, and just throw up my hands in despair...but I won't.

In my roundabout fashion, I'm saying S.W.O.T. doesn't apply to my unusual profession, or my unusual "er" - ME...so I don't use it. Instead, being the creative soul that I am, I've created my own acronym...an acronym to inspire and focus me on my strange, never-ending entrepreneurial venture. Ladies and Gentlemen, I give you "W.A.B.I.D.!"

Specifically, it's WONDER, ATTENTION, BELIEVE in yourself, IMAGINATION, and DON'T lose sight of your dream. Strap yourself in, and I'll run you through it.

WONDER

Never lose your childlike sense of WONDER. This is your inner child's zest for life, curiosity about new things, love of adventure and hunger to learn. If you're in a rut, working a drudge job, it's easy to LOSE your sense of wonder. You're on a schedule, nose to the grindstone, paying the bills. Just the process of getting older can sap away your appreciation for the simple things. You're jaded...seen it all...and you've got no time for it. But as an artist, my sense of wonder is essential to my creativity AND love of life!

Sadly, I have seen incredible artists and writers who "gave up", lost their sense of wonder, and settled for a 9-to-five gig. And I just wonder how many of them later regretted it? I sure would have.

ATTENTION

Pay ATTENTION to what you're doing! Sure, this may seem like the opposite of my previous recommendation, but what can I say? I'm Bi-Polar. There's a time for "wonder", and a time to get down to business! Whenever you don't pay attention, you're likely to MESS UP --giving those who know you the ammunition to verbally humiliate and destroy you time and time again!

Or maybe that's just me.

BELIEVE (in yourself)

This sounds easy enough...and maybe it is for most people. Believe in your abilities, and believe in your choices. If you only allow outside sources to dictate to you, you'll never find self-satisfaction in anything you accomplish. This is co-dependency! It's giving your power to someone else...which, alas, is also something I'm personally familiar with.

NOT believing in your abilities can lead to marrying a co-dependent woman. This leads to exhaustion and depression as you endlessly, hopelessly depend on your partner for your self-worth and self-fulfillment...which leads to increased Bi-Polar mental illness...which leads to your first taste of Lithium!

Or maybe that's just me.

For what it's worth, I got a divorce. Facing the world without my "shield" --my ex-wife-- was a shock to my system...but it was also a chance to grow and take responsibility for myself. I learned to interact better with the world, learned how to fix my own things, make my own meals, and generally take care of my own self. BOY, was that a miracle! I now have belief in myself. I'm a survivor.

IMAGINATION

Don't be afraid to be CREATIVE. Sometimes it seems the world wants to CRUSH your creative side. You're just a cog in the machine...a robot on the assembly line. "But what if there's a better way...?" As an entrepreneur or would-be entrepreneur, you've probably already asked yourself that.

Using your imagination is NOT just for artists. "Thinking outside the box" --while being the most overused catch phrase ever-- has also given us nearly every invention and innovation since the wheel!

"I'm just making this up as I go along" is one of my favorite movie quotes (spoken by Indiana Jones, in *Raiders of the Lost Ark*). It nicely captures what I feel entrepreneurs often have to do...and you shouldn't feel guilty when you do it! When you "make it up"...when you use your imagination to come up with a creative solution...you're not pulling the idea out of nowhere. You're actually accessing the storehouse of information and experiences in your head, and intuitively coming up with a creative solution to your problem!

Granted, your creative solution might be wrong...but don't feel guilty about trying it.

That's just one more mistake you won't have to make again!

DON'T LOSE SIGHT OF YOUR DREAM

IF you start your own business...and IF you become really successful, famous, and/or wealthy because of it...will you still remember WHY you started it? Or will you be distracted and consumed by GREED, CORRUPTION, or LUST for POWER? "Bwah-hah-hah!" (Insert evil laugh here).

Okay, I'm going off on a tangent here. I do that.

I'VE never been "really successful, famous, and/or wealthy." I don't have personal experience with this ...but I HAVE seen a lot of movies and TV, and read a lot of books. I've seen and read about people (real and fictional) who "made it big," but lost their way!

They forgot what was important, their thinking got warped, and their "well of creativity" dried up!

Like the man-eating plant *Audrey II*, from the movie *Little Shop of Horrors*, your initial idea can grow and mutate into something with a mind of its own...and it can CONSUME YOU!

Figuratively, of course. I'm not great with analogies.

The point, again, is to remember the beautiful concept you started with. It seems to me that you'll feel hollow and unfulfilled if you do something just to make money. Making money will, hopefully, be the by-product of your dream business --NOT the reason.

So that's W.A.B.I.D. I would have named it "W.A.B.B.I.T." -- but DARN IT, I couldn't find the words to fit! And that's also a peek into this entrepreneur's strange life.

"Woe is me?" Not hardly.

Sure, my career path is tough. And sure, I'll always have mental health problems, learning disabilities ...and, amazingly, even other issues I haven't mentioned in this article (If we meet sometime, I'll give you an earful!). I could fall back into living my clinical diagnosis, but I choose NOT to...so much so that I haven't had to be hospitalized in over 40 years.

I owe some of that to "going W.A.B.I.D.," and the sentiments behind the acronym!

One last thought: Having a sense of a Spiritually Higher Power gassing You and your Dreams Up helps too. Especially when your fuel gauge reads EMPTY.

Having faith in a power greater than myself helps too! Which I chose to acknowledge as Jesus the Son of our God.

Good luck in all your ventures!

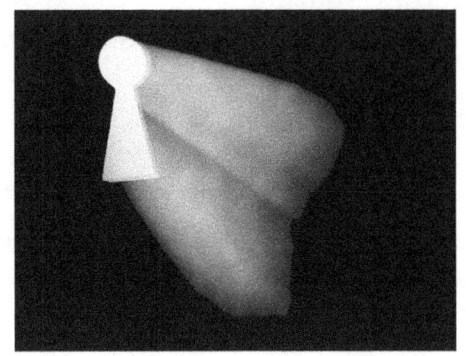

Author Biographies

James Babcock

The name is Babcock. James E. Babcock. And I have a license to THRILL! Which is what I hope to continue doing as someone who has grown tired of what passes for Comics today. Just because it sells doesn't make it right. So I continue with my "three" man art group to crank out as many "Madame X Incorporated," "Dyn-A-Mic Tales" and "Hero Verses Foes Comics" as I possibly can. I am a God Fearing man of "58" who's been living in Tucson, Arizona since the age of eight. My art and stories are a big part of how I see what's occurring in our world today and where I fit in. I am handicapped, but I chose not to live the diagnosis of my illness. So I draw, write, and basically have fun chasing after my STAR! Care to take a look?

Webpage: babcockgraphicspress.com.
Email: toons4u@msn.com

Darrell Parrish Bakeman

Darrell Parrish Bakeman is a native Chicagoan who currently resides in Tucson, AZ. She earned a master's degree in education administration and a bachelor degree in music education with an emphasis in voice. She uses her "voice" powerfully as an organization spokes-person, focus group moderator, host for radio and cable talk-shows and public speaker. Ms. Bakeman believes that being significant is just as important as being successful. Under the banner of "It's a Simple Thing" she works to do just that; as a public speaker, consultant and inspirational expert.

Email: contactitsasimplething@gmail.com

Randy Casarez

Randy Casarez was born and raised in Tucson, AZ. Randy still lives in Tucson, and has four college degrees including Master Degree in Accounting. Randy is a public speaker, and self-published author. Randy wrote his first short story in 2011 called the "The Big Ones." A Fictional story about President George W. Bush sleeping with Jimmy Lopez's girlfriend. Randy has followed politics since he was a kid, and he enjoys writing about real politicians in fictional situations. Randy is writing a fictional story about the 2008 presidential election called "Change Is Within You." When Randy is not writing he enjoys going to Toastmasters meetings. It gives him a chance to work on his public speaking skills, and improve on his leadership skills.

Email: randy_casarez@yahoo.com

Yontaek Choi

Yontaek Choi flew from Korea to Tucson to become a student at the University of Arizona in 1994. He soon found a permanent home there, eventually changing his status from student to alumni, then to employee and parent at the school. He has been working as an IT (Information Technology) staff member since 1999. Yontaek likes traveling through western United States, camping and hiking. When he is not going anywhere, he plays tennis. Yontaek likes to drive so much that he can manage the entire eight hour trip from Tucson to LA in a state of complete joy. He thinks driving can be a happy event, and we can enjoy every day, but only if all drivers are able to respect each other.

Email: yontaek@hotmail.com

Myrna P. Fileccia

At 67, Myrna long ago should have cast aside lesson plans and should now simply be fulfilling her bucket list of traveling, writing and most of all, watching her grandchildren grow. Instead, she decided to give her teaching career one "last hurrah!" To be "just" a classroom teacher, for the next year or so, is Myrna's new personal quest. So, why is a retired Ivy League graduate teaching a class of students with extreme behavior disorders? Does she enjoy being roughed up and investing more resources than she is taking in? This last stretch in Myrna's journey is more than just the "Once a teacher..." syndrome.

Email: myrnaptf2@yahoo.com.

John Grand

Originally from Hudson, New York, John left home in 1955 to join the United States Army as an enlisted man. During his 9th year in the Army he was accepted in the Army Officer Candidate Program, graduating as a 2nd Lieutenant. John served two tours in Vietnam in the Mechanized Infantry Unit over the period of 1967-1968 and 1969. He retired from the United States Army in 1976 with 21 years of service. After retirement John worked for a contractor to train the Saudi Arabian National Guard in Modern Mechanized Infantry Tactics. In 1994, while still in Saudi Arabia, he became a member Toastmasters

International. John currently belongs to three Toastmasters clubs in Tucson, Arizona, his home club Aztec, an advanced club Leaders 1st and a special club he started for U. S. Military Veterans. John currently lives in Green Valley, Arizona with Sylvia, his wife of 35 years.

Email: jgrand5@cox.net

Barb Hildenbrand

Barb Hildenbrand is a mom, grandma, great-grandma, and a foster mom. She is a passionate and loving person who is a firm believer in the power of relationships. Barb conducts workshops, keynote speeches and seminars about relationships, not only those with others, but with self as well. She is also a personal and professional coach. Her caring and concern for others is evident in her writing and her speaking. Barb finds joy in helping others find their joy.

Email: barb.hildenbrand@gmail.com

Thomas Kanspedos

Thomas was born in Pittsburgh Pennsylvania in 1950 and has one older sister Karen. His dad survived the great depression of the nineteen thirties by washing windows. His dad later went on to own a small window washing company. Thomas joined the Army after graduating from high school, and spent a year of duty in Vietnam from 1970-1971 after completing his military obligation he went on to spend the next 35 years as a letter carrier for the post office in Tucson AZ. He is currently married to his wife Rosemary of forty years and has four children and five grandchildren. He enjoys bike riding, bowling, and is a member of Toastmasters and a volunteer with Kairos prison ministry.

Email: tkhealthcarebenefits@hotmail.com

Arthur G. Lohman

Arthur G. Lohman Sr. is a Vietnam Veteran and has been writing poetry since the 1970's and has been an actor for the past twenty-five years. In 1993 the award winning songwriter Don Hecht did a copyright search of his poems and sent him a letter. He wanted to use "This Tattered Envelope" as the lyrics in an album of songs he was producing. Art also wrote and directed a play that was performed at the 90th anniversary of Toastmasters International in Tucson, Arizona. A talented songwriter who was a stranger to Art saw something of value. Art believes each person has a story to tell, you just have to find an appropriate way for you to tell it.

Email: a.lohman@cox.net.

Raleigh Ormerod

Raleigh Ormerod is a trusted advisor to Fortune 500 and startup leaders with innovations delivering global economic and social impact. Known for bringing clarity and positive change, he's launched dozens of products and grown brands in consumer, medical, technology and building product markets. A driving force behind the conception and launch of P&G's Swiffer, Raleigh now consults, mentors, writes and speaks. He currently resides with his wife, two sons and daughter in Tucson who are active in fitness, music and leadership development programs. Having lived and worked across North America, he maintains an abiding interest in US-Canada commerce. Raleigh is a Distinguished Toastmaster, the highest award bestowed by Toastmasters International, recognizing outstanding achievement in both communications and leadership.

Webpage: www.marketaffinitygroup.com
Email: raleigh@ormerod.us

Andres Ruiz

Andres Ruiz is a Life Coach & Speaker that is very passionate about helping people with their health. He is also passionate about motivating the youth so we can have a better future in the world. Ever since joining toastmasters he began pursuing his dream which was to be a motivational speaker. While giving motivational speeches he discovered another niche that peaked his interest, which was life coaching. Andres helps his clients transform their bodies so they can be more confident, healthy and most importantly being happy. Andres is a strong believer in affirmations and is always reminding his family, friends, and clients to always believe in themselves NO MATTER WHAT! His favorite affirmation of them all is I BELIEVE IN MYSELF!!! Contact information:

Webpages: www.h4ltransformativecoaching.com
www.purposemotivator.com
YouTube channels: Life Coach Vida
Purpose Motivator
Email: Lifecoachvida@gmail.com

Philip Schultz

Colonel Philip Lewis Schultz, Command Pilot, United States Air Force (retired) has had many careers, starting with six years as a newspaper delivery boy. His education includes, a Bachelor of Science at Drexel College in engineering, and a Master's in Business Administration (MBA) at the USAF Institute of Technology. He worked four years as an industrial engineer before being recalled to active duty as a C-45 Transport pilot. He was in charge of contracting with three major military bases. After 15 years with Equitable Life & Causality Insurance Company, he retired at 65.

Since retirement, he has been active in Reading Seed, One on One Partners, hosting foreign students, AWANA (an international Christian nonprofit organization founded to help "reach kids, equip leaders and change the world for God"), attending Toastmasters & Lions Club meetings, and participation in many other clubs and organizations.

Email: philiplewisschultz@gmail.com

David Smith

David Smith is a software executive who enjoys reading (absorbs) biographies in his spare time. He loves to play games with his seven kids and wife Kirstin, enjoys cooking and a good glass of wine, and relishes the opportunity to make presentations to various groups on a variety of topics. He, Kirstin and their younger children have a permanent home in Tucson, Arizona, and are on temporary assignment in South

Australia where they enjoy the beach, the Aussies, and driving on the left side of the road.

Email: davidkingsmith@mac.com

Michael Sorantino

Michael Sorantino is a serial entrepreneur, health and fitness guru, and a public speaker. He has a passionate and persistent motivation for the pursuit of living the highest quality life. He believes the key to a fulfilling and high quality life is about a balanced and strong foundation supported by health, wealth, and relationships. He believes that everyone has within them everything they need to get everything they want. Michael makes presentations on the topics of "health and fitness," and "the balanced life."

Email: msorantino@gmail.com

Terry Sprouse

Terry Sprouse is an author, speaker and Lincoln-ologist. Ever since reading Carl Sandburg's "Abraham Lincoln," which fortuitously fell into his hands as a literature-starved Peace Corps Volunteer in Honduras in 1986, he has been captivated and inspired by this legendary figure. Terry now writes books and delivers speeches and seminars to groups about Mr. Lincoln's storytelling, periodically turning up on radio or television interview shows. Terry and his wife, Angy, live in Tucson, Arizona with their two above-average teenage boys.

Webpage: www.TerrySprouse.com

YouTube channel: https://goo.gl/ciXqh6
National Speakers Association page: https://goo.gl/sTGV44
Email: tsx15@hotmail.com

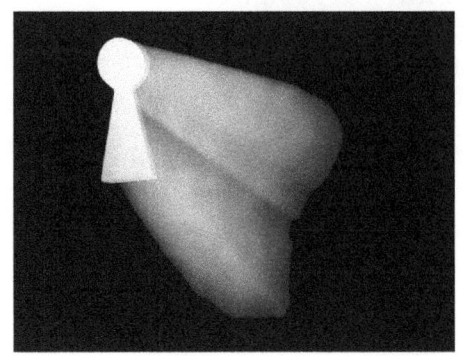

Coming soon!

Keys to Success on the Road Less Traveled, Part II

www.ingramcontent.com/pod-product-compliance
Lightning Source LLC
Chambersburg PA
CBHW020916090426
42736CB00008B/657